MW01093803

The doctrine of divine impassibility has been maligned, misunderstood, unhelpfully nuanced, and even rejected in our day. Why such differing opinions over a doctrine included in the Westminster Confession of Faith and the Second London Confession of Faith (1677/1689)? As this brief book will show, older theologians not only understood the doctrine (and agreed among themselves) but defended it as being taught in the Holy Scriptures. There was a day when this was not a controversial issue among Reformed thinkers. But why is it sorely misunderstood in our day? Though Samuel Renihan does not say it in these words, in *God without Passions: a Primer* his method of approaching the doctrine of divine impassibility is the answer to that question. The reason why divine impassibility is so misunderstood in our day has to do with how we approach the Scriptures, specifically how we interpret them. Though every chapter is worth reading and will provide much profit, if you are like me at all, chapter 1 will seal the deal. In that chapter Sam lists and discusses four hermeneutical principles necessary to use while seeking to interpret biblical texts about God that at first glance seem to be contradictory.

I commend this book to people in the pew, theological students, pastors, and seasoned theologians. It is well-written and easy to digest. Its method is sound. Its doctrine is confessionally and biblically faithful. Its last chapter shows how important and practical the doctrine of divine impassibility is. Though only a "Primer," its contents will inform the mind and fill the soul with wonder and amazement. May you increase in the knowledge of God!

Richard C. Barcellos, Pastor
Grace Reformed Baptist Church
Palmdale, CA
****

The biblical presentation of God who does not change, whose character is eternal, is not a plaything, something merely for the ivory tower. He who is beyond time and change uses representations of himself that are human-like in order to adapt himself to our circumstances, and to be our guide in life. This means that in our thinking about God we are required to discipline our minds, and Samuel Renihan shows us how to do this.

Such thinking deeply affects our approach to the incarnation. Eternal God becomes incarnate not by changing himself, but by condescending. He stoops, taking on our nature. This is the full, rich, and mysterious incarnation, our two-natured Mediator. In commenting on 1 Peter 1:21 Calvin writes that in Christ "God in a manner makes himself little, that he might accommodate himself to our comprehension; and it is Christ alone who can tranquilize consciences, so that we may dare to come in confidence to God."

In Christendom and the wider culture, "there are many 'gods' and many 'lords,' yet for us there is one God, the Father, from whom are all things and for whom we exist, and one Lord Jesus Christ, through whom are all things and through whom we exist . . ." (1 Cor. 8:5-6). The character of this God is to be proclaimed as the faith of the church. So it is a great boon to have a straightforward, clear, and reliable guide for the benefit of the people of God. "This is God, our God, forever and ever. He will guide us forever" (Psalm 48.14).

Paul Helm
Formerly Professor of the History and Philosophy
of Religion
King's College, London, UK
****

Samuel Renihan's *God without Passions: a Primer* provides a clear, cogent, biblical, and pastoral presentation of truth about our all-sufficient, constantly-faithful God. Too often today the truth that the eternal, unchangeable Creator sustains his universe, redeems his people, and interacts with his creatures *without becoming hostage to their ceaseless fluctuations* is ignored, misunderstood, misrepresented, and rejected. Renihan demonstrates the biblical origins and historical foundations of this doctrine, and he shows its positive implications for our personal spiritual struggles and for the pastoral care of our fellow-strugglers.

Dennis E. Johnson
Professor of Practical Theology
Westminster Seminary California
****

In addition to penning extensive theological systems and confessional documents, the theologians of the Reformation and post-Reformation era devoted their energy to writing shorter treatises for the instruction of the church. They did so convinced that theology was *itself* practical (not that it needed to be *made* practical), as it not only nourished faith but promoted the worship and adoration of our infinite God and Savior. Sam Renihan's *God without Passions: a Primer* is clearly born of the same conviction and directed toward the same goal. Drawing upon an impressive range of historical Reformed sources, this work not only retrieves a doctrine that has been unceremoniously left for dead by many, but with theological precision and pastoral warmth teaches us that divine impassibility is a vital biblical truth, one we neglect, modify, or reject to our own theological and spiritual detriment. I cannot recommend this book highly enough, both to those who are unfamiliar with this doctrine and to those who have wrongly assumed that divine impassibility is but a vestige of an unbiblical and impractical theological system for which we have no need. Read carefully and your knowledge of the living God will be deepened, your faith increased, your hope enlivened, and your love warmed.

Stefan T. Lindblad, Pastor
Trinity Reformed Baptist Church
Kirkland, WA
Ph.D. Candidate, Calvin Theological Seminary
****

I really like this book. In the studies and debates for the last few years about God's impassibility, this book would have helped us greatly. When a debate over doctrine begins among theological friends, sometimes the terminology chosen is unfamiliar and provocative, sometimes interpersonal relations affect our reactions to theological statements, sometimes opinions are formed too early to foster real openness in discussion, and sometimes the frustration of the complexity of the subject moves one to settle upon unstudied opinions or side with friends. What Sam Renihan has done in *God without Passions: a Primer* is to provide clarity in terminology and foundational principles for discussing the issue. Especially, he provides a long-needed reminder of the biblical hermeneutics necessary to discuss accurately such a difficult topic. Further, Renihan's insight that God does not have affections or passions but, rather, perfections, is the biblical and theological key often missing in the debate whether God "feels" love, mercy, anger, etc. This has been the wrong question and focus in the debate. The idea of God "feeling" or being "affected" according to man's changing condition is "God with passions." "God without passions" is his always active and unchanging love, compassion, justice, etc., which always affects all men, and all according to his predestined will. God does not "feel" love in reaction to man; rather, he loves actively all the time in his acts toward men. It is God's unchanging essence and attributes which governs his actions in this creation. He is always active but never reactive. The so-called reactive actions of God such as God repenting, grieving, etc., are for us to understand what he is like in his always active attributes. Therefore, he is "without passions." Finally, I commend Sam Renihan in his clear, consistent outline and explanations which are easy to follow on such a complex topic. However, his final chapter on "Personal Applications and Pastoral Implications" catches my attention as the kind of Pastoral Theology we need more of today. I will be using this book with my people.

Fred A. Malone, Pastor
First Baptist Church
Clinton, Louisiana
Author of *The Baptism of Disciples Alone*
****

In this little book, Samuel Renihan has put crucial truth about God on the table for "everyman," including some matters so deep that they challenge faithful pastors to reflect on whether our understanding is truly sound and biblical. Yet for all that, Sam's capable treatment is clear, warm, and conversational.

To use an analogy, *God without Passions: a Primer* is like a wholesome, satisfying meal, nourishing our souls. It should be eaten leisurely, for pleasure and for health, and with gratitude to the impassible God who provides it. The last chapter explaining the practical uses of this theology is a delectable dessert, but let me suggest its use also as an appetizer. If you wonder whether this topic will benefit you as a Christian, then read the last chapter first. Then when you've read the preceding chapters, read it again for maximum impact. With God's blessing, you will never be the same.

Though some of these ideas may seem novel to some readers, they are the sweet fruit of profound study and reflection upon the biblical text, widely enjoyed by the church through the centuries. The modern Christian's typical unfamiliarity with them is an alarming evidence of widespread doctrinal malnourishment.

Let me invite and urge you to put aside any distracting junk food, breathe a prayer of thanksgiving for this feast, and sit down to savor it. The Lord strengthen your inner man by this rich fare!

D. Scott Meadows, Pastor
Calvary Baptist Church (Reformed) of Exeter
New Hampshire
Author of *God's Astounding Grace*
****

Many theological writers can be expected to understand their subject. Far fewer are able to make their subject understandable. Samuel Renihan has that rare ability to do both. This "primer" presents a profound truth in a profoundly simple manner.

Like facets of a diamond, the impassibility of God is viewed: first, with exegetical precision; second, with anthropological illustration; third, with logical consideration; fourth, with theological explanation; and finally, with pastoral application.

I would recommend that the author's *God without Passions: a Reader* be read before this present volume and then again after. The two volumes are complementary.

The doctrine of divine impassibility has suffered from neglect by those who say they believe it and from misrepresentation by those who say they do not. The issue is too important to allow muddled thinking or ambiguous semantics to cloud the discussion.

This book will find use in the hands of scholars and students, pastors in pulpits and people in pews. I have read few modern theological treatments that can both illumine and inspire. The old writers excelled at both and it is good that God is blessing us with young men who can do the same.

David Pitman, Senior Pastor
Addyston Baptist Church
Addyston, OH
****

God Without Passions: a Primer is the most important theological book most Christians don't know they need to read. The theological terrain of divine impassibility is dangerous, often leading to a view of God that is either temperamental or altogether unfeeling. But pastor Sam Renihan leads us safely through to the open pastures of God's true character where certainty and safety abound. This is not an intellectual exercise, nor is this a theological issue divorced from one's faith and experience of God. Rather, these pages help the Christian to find confidence in God's mercy and love—not as mere affections, but as divine perfections. The difference between the two is the difference between a small god and the eternal, triune God of heaven and earth. This is an accessible book, biblically persuasive, and a theologically tight work that is sure to benefit the church at large, and strengthen the faith of those who read it with an aim of understanding, depending on, and worshipping the God who is love.

Joe Thorn, Pastor
Redeemer Fellowship
St. Charles, IL
Author of *Experiencing the Trinity*
****

GOD
without
PASSIONS

A

PRIMER

BY
SAMUEL RENIHAN

Publifhed according to Order.

PALMDALE, CA
Printed by Richard Barcellos for Reformed
Baptift Academic Prefs, **MMXV**

Copyright © 2015 Samuel Renihan. All rights reserved.

Scripture quotations taken from the Holy Bible, English Standard Version® (ESV®), copyright © 2001 by Crossway Bibles, a publishing ministry of Good News Publications. Used by permission. All rights reserved.

Requests for information should be sent to:

RBAP
349 Sunrise Terrace
Palmdale, CA 93551
rb@rbap.net
www.rbap.net

No part of this publication may be reproduced, stored in a retrieval system, or transmitted in any way by any means, electronic, mechanical, photocopy, recording, or otherwise, without the prior permission of RBAP except as provided by USA copyright law.

Printed in the United States of America.

Cover design and formatted for print by Cameron Porter.

ISBN-13: 978-0-9916599-1-3
ISBN-10: 0991659910

Every good gift and every perfect gift is from above, coming down from the Father of lights with whom there is no variation or shadow due to change. (James 1:17)

Contents

Preface 17

Introduction 19

Chapter 1: Impassibility's Foundation 21

Chapter 2: The Human Half of the Equation 35

Chapter 3: Eminence and Negation 49

Chapter 4: Perfections and Incarnation 67

Chapter 5: Personal Applications and Pastoral
    Implications 85

Preface

The Second London Baptist Confession of Faith (2LCF) states that "All things in Scripture are not alike plain in themselves, nor alike clear unto all." Perhaps you find the doctrine of divine impassibility to be one of those doctrines that is less clear or less known to you. This primer is designed to give a simple, clear, and practical presentation of the doctrine of divine impassibility for everyone from the pulpit to the pew. In fact, this material was originally presented as six sermons to Trinity Reformed Baptist Church where I am a pastor.

As you read, you will see how impassibility is drawn from the Scriptures as a whole, how it is then integrated and connected to theology as a system, and how it is applied on personal and pastoral levels. You will find that this book is full of the wisdom and insights of theologians of the past for whom the doctrine of divine impassibility was quite clear. Their clarity and conviction will aid the absorption and digestion of this material for those who are unfamiliar with this topic. Their language has been slightly updated for ease of reading.

It is important to know God and worship him as he has revealed himself to us. This book is offered to supply an important piece of God's self-revelation that, though confessed and treasured by the church throughout the ages, has become unclear due to neglect. I have included study questions in order to highlight key elements of this topic for your own personal thought and to encourage discussion in group studies. It's one thing to hear someone else answer questions. It's another to answer them for yourself. May God use this book to enrich your understanding of him as he has revealed himself in Scripture and to increase your appreciation of the truths the church has confessed throughout history.

Samuel Renihan, Pastor
Trinity Reformed Baptist Church
La Mirada, CA
May 2015

Introduction

This book deals with something that you may have never even heard of, the doctrine of divine impassibility. Impassibility is not a word often used in sermons. Even when people are studying systematic theology, impassibility tends to receive a small amount of attention. So what is it? And why is this important?

Divine impassibility is defined as follows: *God does not experience emotional changes either from within or effected by his relationship to creation.* This is a scriptural truth, and a very important part of our system of theology. In chapter two of our Confession, "Of God and the Holy Trinity," we read the following in paragraph 1:

> The Lord our God is but one only living and true God; whose subsistence is in and of himself, infinite in being and perfection; whose essence cannot be comprehended by any but himself; a most pure spirit, invisible, without body, parts, or passions.

But is this doctrine important? Yes. This is the doctrine of God. If there is a part of theology about which we should be especially careful and sensitive, it should be the doctrine of God. Carl R. Trueman said recently:

> When someone starts to tinker with the doctrine of Scripture, many Christians instinctively feel that something nefarious is being done. But when someone starts to tinker with the doctrine of God, many simply assume that very clever people are engaged in improving the tradition.[1]

---

[1] Carl R. Trueman, "Foreword," in ed. Samuel Renihan, *God without Passions: a Reader* (Palmdale, CA: RBAP, 2015), 16.

A church council condemned the denial of this truth in A.D. 400. "If any shall say or believe, that the deity may be turned, changed, or subject to suffering, let him be accursed."[2]

This topic is also important because there is a great deal of confusion about it in churches today. There is no need to get into the controversy itself other than to state that there is one, and we need teaching on this subject. The key phrase under question is, "without . . . passions." God does not have passions. Some have said that this phrase is unclear. They're not sure what it means. Others have tried to define the terms and then take things in a modified direction.

If you are thinking, "I'm not really sure what that phrase means," then you are not alone. It has become increasingly clear that many in our day are lacking study and knowledge in this area. Given these factors, we can conclude that we need teaching on this subject.

It would be a mistake to jump straight into asserting the doctrine of divine impassibility and defending it. It is one piece in a system of doctrine. It stands upon and connects to many other facets of the doctrine of God. So what we need to do in our study is to build up to it. By doing so, we will appreciate not only the doctrine itself, but also just why it cannot be tampered with. So, to start from the ground up, we need to go where the doctrines grow, the Holy Scriptures.

---

[2] Heinrich Bullinger, *Fiftie Godlie and Learned Sermons, Divided Into Five Decades, Containing The chiefe and principall points of Christian Religion, written in three seuerall Tomes or Sections*, trans. H. I., student in divinity (London: Ralph Newberie, 1587), 695. Bullinger is referring to the first council of Toledo and the sixth and seventh anathemas of its creed. "If anyone should say or believe that the Son of God as God suffered, let him be anathema. If anyone should say or believe that the human Jesus Christ, as a human, was incapable of suffering, let him be anathema." In Latin, "Si quis dixerit atque crediderit, Filium Dei, Deum, passum: anathema sit. Si quis dixerit atque crediderit, hominem Iesum Christum, hominem, impasssibilem fuisse; anathema sit."

Chapter 1

Impassibility's Foundation

The most important question about divine impassibility is whether or not it is the teaching of the Bible. However, proving that it is a scriptural doctrine requires more than word studies and counting texts. As we will notice below, various kinds of texts must be considered. And understanding these texts requires proper interpretive principles.

Scriptural Foundation

As you read the Scriptures, you will find a variety of passages that are important for informing our opinions of this subject. The doctrine of divine impassibility is drawn from these passages. Let's familiarize ourselves with them. We will consider three sets or kinds of verses that deserve our attention on this topic. The first group of passages describes God in the language of human experiences and emotions.

1. Some passages describe God in the language of human experience and emotion.

Let's look at several of them. Genesis 6:6-7 says:

And the L ORD regretted that he had made man on the earth, and it grieved him to his heart. 7 So the L ORD said, 'I will blot out man whom I have created from the face of the land, man and animals and creeping things and birds of the heavens, for I am sorry that I have made them.'

God was sorry, he was grieved in his heart, and he had regrets about making man.

Deuteronomy 9:7-8 is one example of many other passages like it. It says:

Remember and do not forget how you provoked the L ORD your God to wrath in the wilderness. From the day you came out of the land of Egypt until you came to this place, you have been rebellious against the L ORD. 8 Even at Horeb you provoked the L ORD to wrath, and the L ORD was so angry with you that he was ready to destroy you.

First Samuel 15:11 says, "I regret that I have made Saul king, for he has turned back from following me and has not performed my commandments."

Lastly, Jonah 3:10 says, "When God saw what they did, how they turned from their evil way, God relented of the disaster that he had said he would do to them, and he did not do it."

Based on these passages, and there are several more like them, what might we conclude about God? We might conclude that God regrets, experiences grief in his heart, is sorry, repents with sorrow, and can be provoked to wrath. What might stop us from just automatically stating or assuming those things?

2. Other passages of Scripture deny that those very experiences are in God.

Numbers 23:19 says, "God is not man, that he should lie, or a son of man, that he should change his mind. Has he said, and will he not do it? Or has he spoken, and will he not fulfill it?"

First Samuel 15:29 says, "And also the Glory of Israel will not lie or have regret, for he is not a man, that he should have regret."

Malachi 3:6 says, "For I the LORD do not change; therefore you, O children of Jacob, are not consumed."

Lastly, James 1:17 says, "Every good gift and every perfect gift is from above, coming down from the Father of lights with whom there is no variation or shadow due to change."

So, what do we conclude from these passages? We conclude that God does not change his mind, does not have regret, and he does not change, not even in the slightest bit.

These passages seem to contradict the first set, however. And two of them are from 1 Samuel. In verse 11 of chapter 15 God is said to regret, and in verse 29 it says he does not regret. What do we do with these two sets of verses? Well, we have more work to do before we can answer this question. There are more passages of Scripture that will help us to reach a right conclusion. For example, consider the following passages.

3. Other passages describe God in a way that makes it impossible for him to experience affections or passions.

Genesis 1:1 confronts the reader with a fundamental distinction between the Creator and the creature. This distinction is vital and inviolable. Many passages help us to see why this distinction informs the way we think about God's impassibility. Chief among such verses is Exodus 3:14. It says:

> Then Moses said to God, "If I come to the people of Israel and say to them, 'The God of your fathers has sent me to you,' and they ask me, 'What is his name?' what shall I say to them?" 14 God said to Moses, "I AM WHO I AM." And he said, "Say this to the people of Israel, 'I AM has sent me to you.'" (Exod. 3:13-14)

This passage is perhaps the most important one we will read. Keep it bookmarked in your mind.

John 4:24 says, "God is spirit, and those who worship him must worship in spirit and truth."

Lastly, Acts 14:15 says:

> Men, why are you doing these things? We also are men, of like nature with you, and we bring you good news, that you should turn from these vain things to a living God, who made the heaven and the earth and the sea and all that is in them.

Literally Paul says, "We are of the same passions with you."

Now, I am going to assert some things from these verses, and those assertions will be explained more fully later in the book. From these verses we gather at the very least that God is eternal. He does not exist in time. Creation was not, then creation was. God always is. He is eternal.

Furthermore, we gather from the divine name in Exodus 3:14 that God is all that he is. You can't add more to him. You can't take anything away from him. This also means that God is simple. He's not made up of multiple parts. He is what he is, in and of himself.

We gather from John 4:24 that he is spirit, not like angels, but as Creator. He doesn't have a body. He is not subject to the existence that creatures, and especially we humans, know. In fact, if you're Paul and you want to convince a crowd that you're not a god, just tell them that you have the same nature as they do, and you are subject to the same defects and flaws.

What conclusion can we draw from these passages? Well, we need to reconcile them together. Peter Martyr Vermigli said:

> The interpreters labor earnestly to understand how repentance may happen unto God. For God says; I am God, and am not changed. And in the first of Samuel; The triumpher of Israel is not changed. And Balaam in the book of Numbers says; God is not as a man, that he should be changed: neither as the son of man that he should be a liar. Yet in Genesis he says; It repents me that I have made man. Forsomuch as these places seem to be repugnant, they must be accorded together.[1]

We need to understand them in a way that accounts for all of them. This will give us a method of interpretation, a way of looking at the Scriptures, which we are drawing from the Scriptures themselves.

Method of Interpretation

As we reconcile these passages together, principles of interpretation come to the fore. Let's consider four of them.

---

[1] Peter Martyr Vermigli, *The Common Places of the most famous and renowned Diuine Doctor Peter Martyr*, trans. Anthonie Marten (n.p., 1583), 206.

1. Passages that tell us about God's being or nature take priority over passages that describe God's actions.

Passages that tell us that God is not a man, or not like a man, for example, control passages that describe him as a man, physically or emotionally. Think about the two statements in 1 Samuel. On the one hand, God is said to regret, and on the other hand God is said not to regret or to have no regret. Which of the two receives priority? Well, what is the reason given in 1 Samuel for why God does not regret nor has regret? The reason given is that "he is not a man." Because God is a different being, not a man, certain things that are true about man cannot be true of God.

The same is true in Numbers 23:10. It says, "God is not a man, or a son of man." Because of who and what God is, namely God, he cannot undergo the experiences that humans do. The passages that describe God's nature to us control the way that we read passages that describe God in the language of human features and experiences.

Think about this. We do the same thing when we speak in everyday communication. If I say, "Your nose is growing, Pinocchio," is there any doubt in anyone's mind as to whether or not your nose is growing? There's no doubt because we all know, based on what humans are, noses don't grow like Pinocchio's nose grew. But that phrase communicates something to you. It is a figure of speech. If you talk to a skier, and they say, "I was flying down the mountain," is anyone wondering if that skier has wings that they're hiding? No, it's a figure of speech. That brings us to the second principle of interpretation.

2. Scripture uses the physical features and emotional experiences of mankind in order to teach us about God. But we must not equate the human language used to describe God with God himself.

Hugh Binning said:

> Therefore the Lord accommodates himself unto our terms and notions; *balbutit nobiscum*[2] he like a kind father stammers with the stammering children, speaks to them in their own dialect; but withal would have us conceive he is not really such a one, but infinitely removed in his own being from all these imperfections. So when you hear of these terms in Scripture, O beware you conceive God to be such a one, as yourselves: but in these expressions not beseeming his Majesty, because below him; learn your own ignorance of his glorious Majesty, your dullness and incapacity to be such, as the Holy One must come down as it were in some bodily appearance, before you can understand anything of him.[3]

There are two sides to the equation here. And we can end up in two ditches if we are not careful. On the one side, we have to wrestle with the fact that verses that describe God in human form or emotion cannot be taken as one-to-one depictions of God. God is not like us. But in negating such things of God, we have to be careful to make sure we don't forget that these passages are still telling us something.

---

[2] "He stammers with us."

[3] Hugh Binning, *The Common Principles of Christian Religion* (Glasgow: Printed by R.S., 1666), 122-23.

Impassibility's Foundation

God is speaking to us in our language, and we can't equate him with our language, but that doesn't mean that there's nothing for us to learn. It is quite the opposite, in fact.

In another chapter we will dive deeper into this very question, but let me give you a preview. When Scripture speaks of God repenting, regretting, or relenting, why does it say that? The point of connection is not between the emotional state of a human that repents and some emotional state in God, but in the action taken. When someone repents, they stop doing what they were doing, and they begin to do something else. So also, God created man, then he destroyed man, God made Saul king then he removed him, and God threatened judgment on Nineveh, then he removed the sentence of judgment.

You can call that repentance because of the analogy between God's action and human actions, without taking along with it the baggage of human emotional turmoil. When we repent, it is because something confronts us and we are changed. Spiritually speaking, we turn from sin to righteousness. Generally speaking, we encounter some problem, we regret a decision, and we redo something or start over, or do something else. God's existence is not bound by time. Quite to the contrary, God has foreordained whatsoever comes to pass, and he accomplishes all his holy will. So can a simple spiritual God who has decreed all things and cannot be hindered, can that God repent? Not in the sense that we do. But did he decree from all eternity both to create man, and to destroy him, to make Saul king, and then to remove him, to threaten Nineveh, and then to deliver it? Absolutely. And those actions are described to us in human language.

Let's move on to a third principle of interpretation.

3. Human language and understanding cannot contain who and what God is. Revelation may be accommodated to our capacities, but it is not false.

We can no more contain God in our language than you can contain the ocean in a thimble. The finite cannot contain the infinite. Thus our minds and language can never wrap themselves around God and fully express him. Does that mean that when we talk about God, or when Scripture talks to us about God, it is telling us false things? No, it simply means that we have to understand that we are using creature-language to describe an infinite and perfect God, a God who told Moses that no one can see him and live.

John Calvin said, "And although this be spoken according to the weakness of our capacity, yet it is not falsely said."[4] John Weemes echoed, *"Est inadaequatus conceptus sed non falsus*, it is an unequal conception but not false."[5] James Ussher said:

> Thus we speak as well as we can, yet in a broken and imperfect manner to God, as little children speak to their nurses; and Almighty God speaks in a broken and imperfect language to us again, for our weakness and understanding's sake . . . for if the nurse should speak perfectly to the child, as she could to one of greater capacity, the child would not understand her: so if God should speak unto us as he could, and according to his own nature, we were never able to understand him, nor conceive his meaning.[6]

---

[4] John Calvin, *The Institution of Christian Religion*, trans. Thomas Norton (London: Anne Griffin, 1634), 236-37.

[5] John Weemes, *The Portraiture of the Image of God in Man* (London: Printed by T.C., 1636), 87-88.

[6] James Ussher, *A Body of Divinitie, or the Svmme and Svbstance of Christian Religion* (London: Printed by M.F., 1645), 34.

Thomas Hodges speaks similarly:

> So if you read that he is angry, jealous, or the like,
> then know, the Scripture . . . speaks in our dialect;
> and as the nurse in talking with her young one
> brings down her language to the child's conception,
> so God does his; hence comes such low expressions
> in holy writ, because in spiritual things we are very
> dull, but yet we must not think that passions, or such
> things are really in God; but it is because his works
> are such as men's when passions do possess their
> minds; as to destroy, consume, confound, the work
> he has wrought, yet perturbations have no place in
> him.[7]

God's essential glory and infinite perfection are too much for
creatures. We cannot comprehend him. We cannot reach our
arms around the great tree that is God. But we can
apprehend him truly. We can put our hands on the tree and
know it.[8]

The truth of revelation comes from its author, God. And
we must speak of him as he has taught us in his word. So
what do we do? We can speak of him in human language
and terms, but we must not then limit God by thinking we
have contained God in that language, or fully expressed him
as he is. Scripture never speaks falsely to us; it speaks in our
language. It is accommodated. And we need to follow its
lead, its own method of interpretation.

---

[7] Thomas Hodges, *A Glimpse of Gods Glory* (London: Printed for Iohn
Bartlet, 1642), 37-39.

[8] This analogy has often been used to describe the difference between
comprehending (wrapping one's arms around the tree) and apprehending
(placing a hand on the tree).

4. We need to distinguish between our eternal God in himself, and the outworking of his decree in time and space.

God is not limited by time. He is eternal. He created time and transcends it. And everything that God has done, is doing, and will do in time is the fulfillment or the outworking of his decree. God's decree is simple as he is simple. It is one cause, with an unfathomable multitude of effects.

So then, if we ascribe things like emotions to God, or reactions like repenting, relenting, regretting, or being provoked to wrath, we must not understand those as states of being brought about through some successive existence in God. Rather they are the outworking of his eternal and singular decree. Hercules Collins said:

> God's will is not suspended unto time, to see the creatures will before he wills concerning them, as if man's will were to determine his; as if God could not determine his own will until he saw man's. His counsels are called *Counsels of old*, to signify the eternity of them. We poor Creatures will in time; but there is no time with him, all is eternity with him.[9]

Conclusion

So what is the conclusion to our method of interpretation? God is infinite and incomprehensible, but he has made

---

[9] Hercules Collins, *Mountains of Brass, or A Discourse Upon the Decrees of God* (London: John Harris, 1690), 9-10. Collins cites Edward Polhill "upon the Divine Decrees," whom he is quoting. Cf. Edward Polhill, *The Divine Will Considered in its Eternal Decrees, And Holy Execution Of them* (London: Henry Eversden, 1673), 5, 12.

himself known to us by speaking in language that we can understand.

We have arrived at this conclusion by comparing Scripture with Scripture and coming out of that with a unified (and biblical) way of interpreting the Bible. We are thus careful not to equate creaturely language with God while at the same time finding positive teaching and meaning in that creaturely language. We will delve into these things in more detail below. But this lesson is important because it draws the lines, establishes the rules, and clears the playing field. It gives us a theological method, a way of approaching the question.

That God has no passions is an assertion in a huge theological context. It is not an isolated truth. So we are building from the ground up. And if you do your theology right, methodologically, then by the time you get to actually asserting that God has no passions, it makes perfect sense and indeed must be true. But if we start with asserting that God has no passions and try to work backwards, we will get lost and not know where to go because we do not know from whence we have come.

The same applies when we approach our Confession of Faith. If we discuss God being without passions before we discuss everything that precedes it then we are going to be arguing about conclusions with none of the supporting premises. That is an exercise in futility which we would do well to avoid.

May the Lord give us humility to bow before his word, may he give us insight to understand his word, and may he give us love, patience, and charity to teach his word to others. Amen.

Study Questions

1. What are the three kinds of passages described in this chapter, and how do we draw a conclusion about God that is faithful to all three?

2. In our interpretation of the Scriptures, why do we give priority to passages that describe God's being over passages that describe God's actions?

3. What prevents us from drawing a one-to-one connection between human language and God?

4. Is accommodated language false? Why or why not?

5. Though we cannot know God fully, does that mean that we cannot know him truly?

Chapter 2

The Human Half of the Equation

In the first chapter, we covered the exegetical foundations of divine impassibility. We looked at three sets of passages in Scripture: first, verses which describe God in the language of human emotion; second, passages which deny that such emotions are in God; and third, other passages that describe God in such a way that makes it impossible for him to experience affections and passions as we do. We also laid out some ground rules, or some building blocks, for approaching this issue.

First, God is incomprehensible. We can no more contain God in our understanding and language than a thimble can contain an ocean. However, though we cannot comprehend God fully, we can apprehend him truly. We can know God because he has revealed himself to us in our language. Second, we noted from Scripture passages that God is described in the language of human emotions while at the same time Scripture denies that God has those emotions. And third, Scripture's description of God teaches us how to speak about him. We cannot run from the creature to the Creator with a one-to-one correlation. This brings us to the present chapter. If you had questions due to the last chapter, hopefully this chapter will begin to answer them.

So here is the main question or problem that arises from our previous study: If Scripture describes God in the language of human emotions, and then we begin to take away from the meaning of that language, what is left over? In other words, if Scripture says that God regretted something, but he actually does not regret, or cannot regret, what is Scripture telling us in such passages? That is an excellent and important question.

The solution to this question is straightforward, but we have to take time to build it up. So where do we begin? Well, we must remember that confessing that God is "without . . . passions" is a statement about God in which something creaturely is denied to him. Thus, to understand the phrase we need a sufficient understanding of the creaturely nature being denied of God, and the divine nature of which such a negation is necessary. Passions are something creaturely, so in order to understand them we have to begin with the nature of man.

The Nature of Man

Man is a created being. And it is important that we understand man as having parts and faculties.

1. The parts of human nature

With respect to parts, God has created man as body and soul. In Genesis, God creates Adam's body from the dust of the ground, then breathes life into him. The body is the material part of man, and the immaterial element is the soul, which will never die.

We are composite creatures, made up of different things, most fundamentally body and soul. But within our bodies and souls we are made up of even more parts. Seated in our body and soul are faculties. God has given us a mind, will, and affections. Let's consider the faculties of human nature.

2. The faculties of human nature

The mind and the will are seated in the soul. If you ask me to show you my mind, or my will, I cannot produce a physical entity. I cannot materialize my thoughts or my knowledge. And I cannot materialize my will, either. The will is the faculty by which we make decisions and take actions. These things are immaterial because they are faculties seated in the soul.

Now, though the mind and will are immaterial and seated in the soul, our bodies play a part in how those faculties take action. So, for example, we have a much better understanding than our forefathers of the brain. The mind or understanding works itself out in the brain. When the brain is damaged, one's understanding is affected. And when we are thinking or dreaming, etc., our brains are active. So the spiritual faculties work themselves out in the body. When we will to do something, we carry out that action with our bodies. The will may be immaterial, but the body is involved. That brings us to affections.

We are going to define the affections, and I want you to pay close attention to the way that the affections are *the meeting place of man's parts and faculties*. We are going to see the body and the soul and the mind and the will involved.

Defining Affections and Passions

1. Affections

Let's read two simple definitions of the affections. Edward Leigh defines the affections as "Certain powers of the soul by which it works and moves itself with the body to good and from evil."[1] William Bridge offers a similar definition. He says, "Affections in the general are these movings of the rational soul, whereby the heart is sensibly carried out upon good or evil; so as to embrace the one, or refuse the other."[2] Both definitions combine the soul, body, and faculties of man. The affections are the actions of the whole man (i.e., parts and faculties), relative to an external object which it perceives as good or bad.

Let's take some time to examine these definitions closely. Notice the language of the soul "working and moving itself" or the "movings of the rational soul." A man with affections has the capacity to move himself, rationally and volitionally, that involves the mind and the will. But the way that man takes action is through the body, as Edward Leigh mentions. And William Bridge mentions that the heart is sensibly moved. There is a physical action or reaction involved. Now, why would someone move themselves? Well, these definitions say that the affections are when we encounter something good or evil, and then we take action relative to how we perceive it. In Leigh's definition, we will move *towards* good and *away from* evil. In Bridge's definition, we *embrace* good or *refuse* evil.

Think about that. Mankind is endowed with the natural capacity to encounter things, to evaluate them as good or evil, and then to act accordingly. Those are affections. And if the definition seems abstract, consider the following list of affections drawn from Reformed writers: *love, hatred, desire, abomination, joy, sorrow, hope, despair, boldness, fear, anger, error, zeal,* and *pity.*[3]

The first ten are in an order that shows opposites. For example, if you encounter an object, you must perceive it as

[1] Edward Leigh, *A Systeme or Body of Divinity* (London: Printed by A. M. for William Lee, 1662), 758.

[2] William Bridge, *Bridge's Remains, Being VIII Sermons* (London: Printed by John Hancock, 1673), 26.

[3] This is not an exhaustive list, but it is a very representative one.

good or evil. You will use your mind or understanding to do this. And then, if you perceive it to be good, you will love it. If you perceive it to be evil, you will hate it. Likewise, you will desire good, and be repulsed by evil. You will be joyful relative to good, and sorrowful relative to evil. You will hope for good, and despair in evil. You will be bold towards good, and fearful towards evil.

These are the affections. With our body and soul, and the faculties seated in them, mind, will, and affections, we interpret the world around us as good or evil, and we take action based on our perceptions. They are called affections because we are *affected* by something else. We take action based on some external object. John Owen says:

> [Affections] have their dependence on that, wherewith he, in whom they are, is affected; that is, they owe their rise & continuance to something without him, in whom they are. A man's fear arises from *that*, or *them*, of whom he is afraid; by them it is occasioned, on them it depends; whatever affects any man, (that is the stirring of a suitable Affection) in all that frame of mind, and soul, in all the volitions and commotions of will, which so arise from thence, he depends on something without[4] him. Indeed our being affected with something without, lies at the bottom of most of our purposes and resolves.[5]

What are the affections, then? They are the motions of the soul worked out through the body, relative to perceived good or evil. They depend on an external object.

---

[4] "Without" means "outside of."

[5] John Owen, *Vindiciae Evangelicae Or, The Mystery of the Gospell Vindicated, and Socinianisme Examined* (Oxford: Printed by Leon. Lichfield, 1655), 74-75.

Understanding affections is necessary for understanding passions because passions are either equated with affections or they are considered as a subset of the affections.

2. Passions

Now, with all of this ground work, we can finally get to passions. As you can see, it is not safe to dive into this subject without a familiarity with the concepts and categories that it fits in. So then, what are passions? There are two ways to handle them.

The first option is to treat passions *synonymously* with affections. Replace the word "affections" with passions, and you're good to go. For many authors, they are one and the same. And many authors specifically say that they are the same thing. Given that being affected means that something external to you is *affecting* you, it is not surprising to call them passions. Why? Because the root of the word "passions" means that you are being *passive* or that you are suffering. In other words, the individual is affected, or is passive. William Fenner states:

> The affections are the passions of the soul. When the heart is affected with a thing, it lets in that thing, and it suffers a change by that thing; when a man is affected with anger at a wrong or injury, we say he is in a passion; that is, he lets in the wrong, and there does his heart bite upon the wrong, and chase at it; thus he is passionate, when a man is affected with

love to a pleasure, he lets in the pleasure, and suffers it to prevail on the heart.[6]

There are many other examples of authors who treat affections and passions in exactly the same way. They consider them to be synonymous.

The second option is to distinguish passions as a subset of the affections in the context of intensity and irrationality or corporeal change. For example, to love is an affection, but to lust is a passion; to be angry is an affection, but to rage is a passion; and to be sad is an affection, but to be overwhelmed by sorrow is a passion. The intensity of the affection makes it a passion and presupposes an irrationality or loss of control on the part of the individual. A man in lust, rage, or heartbrokenness is not in control of himself. Anthony Burgess said, "These passions have several names, sometimes they are called perturbations, but that is most properly, when they have cast off the dominion of reason."[7] Nicholas Mosely said, "when [affections] grow heady, sensual, fleshy, & terrene . . . these are they which are properly called Passions."[8]

For an example of passions considered as affections that cause a change in the body, Edward Leigh said, "They are commonly called passions . . . because they imprint some passion on the body by working."[9] Authors sometimes give the examples of a rapid pulse, a hot head, trembling, or

---

[6] William Fenner, *A Treatise of the Affections* (London: Printed by R.H., 1642), 12. Cf. "*Passion, is a motion of the sensitive appetite, stirred up by the apprehension, either of good or evill in the imagination, which worketh some outward change in the body.*" Weemes, *The Portraitvre of the Image of God in Man*, 139.

[7] Anthony Burgess, *A Treatise of Original Sin. The First Part.* (London: n.p., 1658), 327.

[8] Nicholas Mosley, *Psychosophia: Or, Natural & Divine Contemplations of the Passions & Faculties of the Soul of Man* (London: Printed for Humphrey Mosley, 1653), 9.

[9] Leigh, *A Systeme or Body of Divinity*, 758.

other physical responses connected to anger, fear, lust, etc., as indicators of passion in contrast to affection. The connection is *physical*. Our *bodies* undergo some change, whether that is bodily harm or simply the affects of fear, lust, anger, and other such passions.[10]

So then, the passions are treated in two ways, either synonymously with affections, or as a subset of the affections in the context of violating the boundaries of nature, reason, morality, etc.

Notice how far into the outline of this chapter this section is. It falls under many other headings: the nature of man, the faculties of man, the affections of man, the passions of man. That is intentional. It shows that we cannot jump into this discussion without doing the groundwork to understand passions in their natural context.

Another helpful dimension of understanding affections and passions is that we have to remember the effects of the fall on human nature.

3. The effects of the fall on human nature

Our Confession of Faith, in the chapter on sin and the fall of man, states that due to our fall in Adam, we are "wholly defiled, in all the faculties, and parts, of soul, and body." Our parts and faculties are sinful, not in the sense that they are the most sinful they possibly could be, but rather there is no part of who and what we are that is untouched by the curse of sin.

This means that our bodies decay and die a physical death. It means that our souls, which will last forever, will not enjoy eternal life but suffer eternal death. It means that

---

[10] This includes the idea of physical harm. The passion of Christ refers primarily to the bodily damage he experienced, though it also includes the anguish of his soul as well.

our mind, our understanding, is darkened. We suppress the truth and believe lies. It means that our will is enslaved to sin. We disobey God's law rather than obeying it.

Given those factors, remember the definition of affections. The affections are the actions of the whole man (parts and faculties) relative to an external object which it perceives as good or bad. If the whole man is defiled in his parts and faculties, unable to rightly process good and evil, and indeed inclined to do evil, what will become of his affections? They are polluted and sinful. We love evil, and hate good. We rejoice in evil and shun good. We hope for sinful things and despair over good things. We fear righteousness and holiness, and act boldly in sin. Our affections violate the boundaries of natural order, morality, and reason. We place them on the wrong objects, and without any measure of limitation or moderation.

In Adam, before the fall, with right reason and an obedient will, his affections were never outside the boundaries of their designed and natural purposes. And so also in Jesus Christ, according to his human nature, he had affections, but they were never outside of control, never immoral, never irrational. But we sinful creatures, how we toss and turn from this affection to that, thrown about on the seas of life!

Conclusion

Let's bring this to a conclusion. Take a moment to review the material we have covered. The problem we have stated is that Scripture describes God in the language of human affections and passions, but we have been negating things about those statements, saying that you cannot treat them one-to-one between God and human experience. And to help resolve the problem or question, we need to understand the human nature that is being denied of God, and the divine nature that makes such a negation necessary. This whole chapter has been dedicated to understanding the human half of the equation.

Think about it with me. Even though we have not covered the divine half of the equation, the nature of God, can we say that God has passions? How do we define them? Does God have affections gone bad, affections that violate moral order, nature, or reason? Of course not. That is impossible. Taken as extreme, uncontrolled, provoked affections, God is without passions.

But what about when we defined passions synonymously with affections? Does God have motions of the soul worked out through the body relative to perceived good or evil? No. Affections and passions, with this definition, may not necessarily be *sinful*, but they are *creaturely*. Does God encounter things, evaluate them, and act accordingly? Is God limited by time, figuring things out as he goes? Or has he decreed all things, whatsoever comes to pass? And can anything God purposes be obstructed, prevented, or changed? Does God change? You see, whether you take passions as a subset of the affections, or as synonymous with affections, God cannot have them. And this is why, when Scripture describes God to us in the language of creaturely affections and passions, we cannot treat it as a one-to-one correlation. God is not like us.

This brings us back to our question of, what is left? With so many negations, does that mean that God has no love, mercy, or anger? Well, to give you a preview of the next chapter, the answer is found in clearing away creaturely imperfections from God in order to see his divine perfections shine forth even brighter. God does not have love, God *is* love (1 John 4:8). God does not have mercy, God *is* merciful (Eph. 2:4). God does not have joy, God is eternally blessed (1 Tim. 6:15). You see, for creatures, these things are qualities; they can be added or subtracted, increased or decreased, provoked or extinguished. But not so in God. Thomas

Adams said, "They are perfections in him what are affections in us."[11]

My dear reader, this is what makes impassibility such a wonderful doctrine. It causes us to recognize our creaturely frame, so changeable and weak. And it causes us to see the essential unchanging perfection of our God. You can wake up and not feel very loving towards others. And they may wake up and find that you are not feeling very loving. You have bad days. You have mood swings. You have temper tantrums. You have depression. You have fear, worry, anxiety, stress, bitterness, resentment, and more. You are constantly being overcome by all sorts of things, outside of you. But it is not so with God. He is all that he is. He is "I am that I am." He is the one who does not change. He is not a man, nor a son of man.

So, love in God is not a passion or affection, but an unchanging perfection. Mercy in God is not like human mercy. Our mercy is heart misery towards another. But we are more prone to be moved by a picture of puppies and kittens than we are to help our neighbor. God, on the other hand, without the passion of mercy, without the heart misery of human feeling, is the God who helps the helpless. He is the one who helps those who can give absolutely nothing back to him, and who do not deserve his help. He is truly merciful.

In the final chapter we will cover several of the pastoral and personal applications that flow from this doctrine, but I hope that this helps you to see how wonderful a doctrine this is. Rather than giving us a picture of an apathetic uncaring God of whom we know nothing, and cannot possibly relate to, we see divine unchanging perfections, which become the very foundation for our running to God. I can wake up every day, and go to sleep every night, knowing that when I cry out to God, I am crying out to the

---

[11] Thomas Adams, *The Workes of Tho: Adams* (London: Printed by Tho. Harper, 1629), 258.

The Human Half of the Equation

God who is love, who is merciful, who is kind. He is all that he is. And we should praise him that he is not like us. We should rejoice that God is without passions.

God does not have a stomach that grumbles, or arms that tire, or legs that tremble, or a mind that needs caffeine, or a head that aches, or a heart that races. He does not have lust, or violent rage, or depression, or fear, or anxiety. God is love. God is mercy. God is holiness. He is a most pure spirit, invisible, without body, parts, or passions.

Let us love God, with rightly ordered affections, and let us praise our God who *is* love. Amen.

The Human Half of the Equation

Study Questions

1. What are the parts of human nature?

2. What are the faculties of human nature?

3. What are affections?

4. What are passions?

5. Given the definitions of affections and passions, are affections or passions in God?

Chapter 3

Eminence and Negation

As we continue with our short study of divine impassibility, we need to make sure that we pick up where we left off. We need to keep in mind the points that we have been making in the first two chapters. In the first chapter, we went to the Scriptures and laid out some ground rules for our study. For one thing, we drew a complete distinction and division between the Creator and the creature. And we drew from this certain necessary principles such as the fact that although Scripture describes God in the language of human emotions, we cannot draw a one-to-one correlation between God and that language. God does not experience affections and passions.

This of course raises the question of what those passages mean. So, in the second chapter, we began to answer the question. And we brought to the forefront the fact that saying that God is without passions requires us to understand two things. We have to understand the human nature that is being denied of God, and we have to understand the divine nature that requires such a negation. So we dedicated a chapter to the human half of the equation, understanding human nature.

As we discussed human nature, we looked at man's parts, body and soul, and his faculties seated in those parts, mind, will, and affections. Then we defined affections. They are the motions of the soul worked out through the body, relative to perceived good or evil. We encounter something, we perceive it as good or evil, and then we react to it.

After that, we defined passions. Passions are either the same as affections, or they are a subset of the affections, when they violate the boundaries of reason, nature, and moral order. So we talked about love becoming lust, or anger becoming rage, or sadness becoming depression.

In all of these definitions we noted how passions and affections bring the parts and faculties of man together. The body and soul, mind and will, are all involved. And affections and passions depend on external objects changing us or affecting us. With all our definitions in place, understanding passions in the context of human nature, we asked the question, does God have passions? And we said, "of course not." This pushed us back to our other question, then what *does* he have, and why does Scripture speak of God in the language of passions and affections? And we concluded by hinting at this chapter, that what are *affections* in us, are *perfections* in God. Clearing away passions from God does not leave him as a cold, numb rock, but rather causes his essential perfections to shine forth.

This chapter picks up where we left off and considers the divine nature of God. When we understand passions in the context of human nature, we say "of course God does not have them." So also, when we understand passions in the context of the divine nature, we say "of course God does not have them." So, let's study the divine nature. To do so, we are going to ask a series of questions. The first of those questions is: *What is God?*

What is God?

What is God? No one knows. No one can know. Why? Well, how do we know things? We know them by comparing one thing to another, and sorting and classifying. That is a dog. That is a cat. We sort them into kingdoms, phyla, classes, orders, families, genii, and species. Can you sort God into some higher class of existence? Is there a genus of which God is the species? Is there a category in which you can place God? No. So what is he? Well, the finite cannot comprehend the infinite.

1. We do not know God in his essence.

We cannot know God as he is in himself, in his essence, outside of creation. Heinrich Bullinger said it well:

> Say all of him whatsoever you can, and yet you shall still rather name some thing of his, than himself. For what can you fitly speak or think of him, that is greater than all your words and senses? . . . What can you fitly think of him, that is above all loftiness, higher than all height, deeper than all depth, lighter than all light, clearer than all clearness, brighter than all brightness, stronger than all strength, more virtuous than all virtue, fairer than all fairness, truer than all truth, greater than all greatness, mightier than all might, richer than all riches, wiser than all wisdom, more liberal than all liberality, better than all goodness, juster than all justice, and gentler than all gentleness. For all kinds of virtues must needs be less than he, that is the father and God of all virtues: so that God may truly be said to be such a certain Being, as to which nothing may be compared. For he is above all that may be spoken.[1]

We cannot know God in his essence. It is impossible. But, that does not mean we can know nothing about God. Rather, it tells us one thing, that God is pure essence. All that is in God is God. We will discuss this further.

---

[1] Bullinger, *Fiftie Godlie and Learned Sermons*, 606-07.

Eminence and Negation

2. God is all that he is, simple spiritual essence.

Do you remember what I said about Exodus 3:14 and the divine name of God? I said that it is perhaps the most important verse in these discussions. Bullinger has more to say.

> Among all the names of GOD that is the most excellent, which they call Tetragrammaton . . . IEHOVAH, that is to say, Being, or I am, as he that is *autousia*,[2] a Being of himself, having his life and Being not of any other, but of himself, lacking nobody's aid to make him to Be, but giving To Be unto all manner of things, to wit, eternal God, without beginning and ending, in whom we live, we move, and have our Being. To this do those words especially belong, which we find to have passed betwixt God and Moses in the third chapter of Exodus: And Moses said to God, Behold, when I come unto the children of Israel . . . and they shall ask me, saying, What is his name? What answer shall I make them? And God said to Moses, I am that I am, or I will be that I will be . . . That is, I am God that will be, and he has sent me, who is himself Being, or Essence, and GOD everlasting.[3]

And John Mayer (not the musician) says:

> Again, I say a spiritual essence *Exod.* 3.14. *I am that I am*, says the Lord, in Hebrew *Ehyeh* from whence comes *Iehovah,* and the name *Iah,* by which we are bidden in the Psalms to praise him. He has essence or being of himself, as none other spirit has, and gives

---

2 "Autousia" means "self-being," which Bullinger explains as he continues.

3 Bullinger, *Fiftie Godlie and Learned Sermons*, 608.

being to all things. There was a time, when the heaven could not say, I am, or earth, or angel, but not at any time, when God could not say, *I am*. And this essence I call simple, because it is undivided, the wisdom of God is not a divers thing from his essence, but the same; *quicquid in Deo est, Deus est*.[4]

There is so much going on here. Drawing from Exodus 3:14, the divine name of God, and John 4:24, where Jesus says that God is spirit, these authors are concluding that God is pure being. He is that he is. There are many interconnected ideas at play here. Because God is what he is, he is *simple*. God does not have parts. He is not a composite being. You cannot add anything up in God that constitutes his existence. He simply is. That is why you cannot classify God in any category. There is no higher cause dictating God's being. And this must be so because any composition, any time two things are put together, implies a higher cause governing the composition. God cannot be God if he is caused. Thus God is simple, spiritual essence. He is not becoming. He is pure being.

Many of the authors will go on to speak of God as "Pure Act." As creatures, we move from potentiality to actuality. We become what we were not. I am able to get stronger, weaker, nicer, meaner, smarter, dumber, and more. I have the potentiality to actualize myself or be actualized in any number of ways. But God is I am that I am, pure being, pure act.

Now I want to show you how the Confession of Faith summarizes these things. It states, "The Lord our God is but one only living and true God; whose subsistence is in and of himself, infinite in being and perfection; whose essence cannot be comprehended by any but himself; a most pure spirit . . ." God is one. There is no other god. He is living. He

---

[4] John Mayer, *The English Catechisme Explained* (London: Printed by Miles Flesher, 1635), 96-97. "Whatever is in God, is God."

Eminence and Negation

is not an idea, or a philosophical construct. He is not a principle. He is true. He is not a figment of man's imagination or invention. Then it says that his "subsistence is in and of himself." Subsistence in this case refers to a mode of existence, or *how* God exists. God exists in and of himself. His existence is not derived from or dependent upon anything else. He is a most pure Spirit. That is, he is not composed of anything, he is all that he is. He is simple.

These are very strong and important statements about our Creator. And they are all drawn directly from Scripture. I would encourage you, on your own time, to look at the Scripture references in the Confession on these points.[5]

Having asked the question, "what is God?," we have given the best answer that we can. While acknowledging that we cannot know God in his essence, we acknowledge at the same time that God is pure essence, that he has revealed himself to us in his divine name and spirituality as the one who is that he is, the one true living God who exists of and for himself.

But we can proceed further in our questions. We can know more about God. But how?

How Can We Know God?

We can know God by his names and by his attributes.[6]

---

[5] 1 Cor. 8:4-6; Deut. 6:4; Isa. 48:12; Exod. 3:14; John 4:24; 1 Tim. 1:17; Deut. 4:15-16; Mal. 3:6; 1 Kings 8:27; Jer. 23:23-24; Psalm 90:2. See the end of the chapter for their texts.

[6] These are not the only ways in which we can know God. This is simply a narrowing of the focus at hand. To mention some of the other ways, we also know him by his works and through the *via causalitatis*, the way of causation.

1. Knowing God by his names

We have already begun this process. We looked at Exodus 3:14 and John 4:24 and we drew from those certain conclusions about God. As in our first chapter, God taught us how to speak of him. But God gives us other names in the Scriptures. Edward Leigh says:

> For the ten Hebrew Names of God (having handled them in another place) I shall say but little of them here. The Name *Jehovah, Jah, Ehejeh* signify Gods Perfect, Absolute and simple Being, of and by himself. Such a Being as gives Being to other things, and upon whom they depend. Such a God as is true and constant in his Promises, ready to make good whatsoever he has spoken. His Name *El, Elohim, Schaddai, Adonai,* signify a God All-sufficient in himself, strong and powerful, able to bless, protect and punish.[7]

Now, it is from these names, which God has given to us (and not the other way around), that we begin to see the attributes of God. This is all drawn from the Scriptures.

2. Knowing God by his attributes

As we come to the attributes of God, we cannot handle each and every one. So let me make a few comments about God's attributes. God does not have attributes. God *is* his attributes. God is all that he is. He is not the sum total of his parts. He is one simple spiritual being. John Norton says:

---

[7] Leigh, *A Systeme or Body of Divinity*, 159.

Eminence and Negation

All the Attributes in God are one and the same Perfection. It is better said of God that he is his Attributes, then that he has Attributes: The Attributes are not distinguished in God, but in our manner of understanding, who being unable to comprehend that mere act at once, do conceive thereof after the manner of many acts. . . . For every and all the Attributes are the divine Essence itself; according to that received Proposition, *Whatsoever is in God, is God*.[8]

This does not erase God's attributes, it simply reminds us to exercise care and caution when we *attribute* something to God. For us, attributes are qualities that can be added or subtracted. Consider this example. The wall is white. It could be painted blue. Then it would be a blue wall. God is not a good God who could become a bad God. His goodness is not a quality. It is an essential perfection. None of his attributes are qualities. He is his attributes. He is all that he is, essentially, perfectly, infinitely, eternally, and immutably. Remember that he is pure act. He has no passive potentiality which could be actualized. He is all that he is, simply. We attribute things to God in order to gain an understanding of his nature.

So then, if we are forced to describe a simple, spiritual, unchangeable, perfect God in the language of little ever-changing creatures like us, how do we attribute things to God? As Bullinger said, if we call him light, we name a created thing, not God. So then, what we do is we use the way of negation and the way of eminence.

---

8 John Norton, *The Orthodox Evangelist* (London: Printed by John Macock, 1654), 3-4. Remember the Latin? *Quicquid est in Deo, Deus est.*

Eminence and Negation

3. Knowing God by the way of negation

The first thing that we do is that we scrub our language clean of anything and everything that does not fit with or agree with the nature of God. We *negate* whatever is inconsistent with God's being. Thomas Taylor helps us out. He describes the way of negation as follows:

> To rise from the Creature to the Creator, *per viam negationis,*[9] when whatsoever is imperfect, disordered or defective in the creature, all that is denied and removed from God, as mortality, passion, change, finiteness, so we call God immortal, infinite, impassible, immutable, &c.[10]

Notice that we are moving from the creature to the Creator. We are using things about us to describe what God is. So in order to know God, we start by saying what he is *not*. This is the primary way in which we know God. Stephen Charnock adds:

> This way of *negation* is more easy; we better understand *what God is not*, than *what he is*; and most of our knowledge of God is by this way; as when we say God is infinite, immense, immutable, they are negatives; he has no limits, is confined to no place, admits of no change. When we remove from him what is inconsistent with his being, we do more strongly assert his being, and know more of him when we elevate him above all, and above our own capacity.[11]

---

[9] "By the way of negation."

[10] Thomas Taylor, *The Works of that Faithful Servant of Jesus Christ, Thom. Taylor, Catechistical Exercises* (London: Printed by T.R., 1653), 52-53.

[11] Stephen Charnock, *The Works of the late Learned Divine Stephen Charnock*, vol. 1 (London: Printed for Ben. Griffin, 1684), 113-14.

When we come to God through the way of negation, we say that he cannot die, he cannot be bounded or limited by anything, and he cannot be subject to motions of the soul worked out through the body relative to perceived good or evil, and he cannot change. Do you see what just happened? We finally hit impassibility in its natural context in theology.

Look at how our Confession of Faith proceeds where we left off. God is a most pure spirit, and because of that, he is, "invisible, without body, parts, or passions, who only has immortality, dwelling in the light which no man can approach unto; who is immutable, immense, eternal, incomprehensible . . ." Those are all negations. And those negations are necessary based upon what God is, which has already been asserted in the Confession, "a most pure spirit."

The Confession follows a very natural progression. If God is "a most pure spirit," a singular, simple, spiritual, purely actual essence, then not only is he "invisible," but he is also "without body." He thus is "without . . . parts." He is not composed of matter and form, body and soul. And if he has no parts, then he does not have separate faculties of will, understanding, or sensation seated in those parts, distinct from his essence. He is "a most pure spirit." Given these truths, it is the most natural and logical of steps to say that God is "without . . . passions."

If you want to understand impassibility, then you need to understand the way of negation. And if you want to follow the way of negation properly, then you need to understand, on the one hand, the human nature that must be denied of God and the divine nature that requires such a negation. Let's move on to the way of eminence.

4. Knowing God by the way of eminence

Speaking of God and his attributes is more than just negations. While the path from the creature to the Creator will almost always be taken with some kind of negation or qualification, where we removed things from God, there will also be times where we see a virtue in us that originates in God and is a perfection of his nature. Thomas Taylor helps us out again. He says:

> A man may safely rise from the creature to the Creator, *per viam eminentiae*,[12] when whatsoever is most eminent in the creature, and nearest to perfection, is attributed by a kind of similitude unto God, as wisdom, love, mercy, justice, holiness, and the like; but so as these must not be conceived qualities in God, as they are in the creature, but of his essence, for *Nihil est in Deo, nisi Deus . . .*[13]

Notice a few important things with me. First, we attribute such things by a *similitude*. That is, there is an analogy. God does not have the same wisdom, love, and mercy, etc., that we have. Second, this means that God has such things according to what he is; in other words, not as qualities which can be removed or added, increased or decreased, but essentially, eternally, and perfectly.

Zanchius will help us understand how this works. He says:

> Although almost all the names of God in the word, are taken from creatures, yet in those names must we consider two things. First the things, or the perfections signified by those names; secondly the manner how these names signify this perfection. As for the things and perfections signified by these names, as they were first, and are in God, and that in a more perfect manner then in the creatures, and by this means proper to God: so also the names

---

[12] "By the way of eminence."
[13] Taylor, *Works*, 52. "Nothing is in God, but God."

themselves, in as much as these perfections are signified by them, are more properly attributed to God then to the creatures; indeed do agree and are affirmed of him before any creature. . . . If then we regard the manner of signifying, they do not so properly belong to God as to us; because that which they signify is after an imperfect manner: therefore we shall make them more properly to belong to God, if we add some such words as doth increase the signification of these names, and so distinguish betwixt God and the creatures; as if that we call God *most just, most wise, most mighty*: for by this shall we put a difference betwixt the imperfect justice of man, & the perfect and essential justice of God.[14]

Zanchius is saying that if we say that God loves, then we are speaking of God in creaturely language. God loves. Man loves. So what we need to do is realize that love is first in God, as a perfection. God *is* love. So how can we, in our language, show that God's love and man's love are not the same, but rather God's is original, perfect, essential, unchangeable, and eternal? We add the word "most." If something is the most, can it be any more? No. If it is the most, can it be any less? No.

Now look at our Confession of Faith at 2.1 again. God is

almighty, every way infinite, *most* holy, *most* wise, *most* free, *most* absolute; working all things according to the counsel of his own immutable and *most* righteous will for his own glory; *most* loving, gracious, merciful, long-suffering, abundant in goodness and truth, forgiving iniquity, transgression, and sin; the rewarder of them that diligently seek

---

[14] Girolamo Zanchius, *Life euerlasting: Or, The True Knowledge of One Iehovah, Three Elohim, and Iesus Immanvel*, ed. Robert Hill (Cambridge: Printed by Iohn Legat, 1601), 10-11.

him, and withal *most* just and terrible in his judgments, hating all sin, and who will by no means clear the guilty. (2LCF 2.1, italics added)

This is what we have to trumpet, loud and clear, on this topic. People hear all the negations and they think that there is nothing left. But through the way of eminence we see God's perfections shining forth. Reformed theology, and the Confessions that summarize it, may deny passions to God, but this is not to transform him into a numb, heartless God. To the contrary, Edward Leigh gives us an encouraging reminder.

The Attributes of God are Everlasting, Constant and Unchangeable, for ever in him, at one time as well as another. . . . This may minister comfort to God's people; God's attributes are not mutable accidents, but his very Essence: His Love and Mercy are like himself, Infinite, Immutable and Eternal.[15]

God is loving, merciful, just, good, and more. He is these things by his very essence, unchangeably and eternally. All of the actions of God that creatures perceive in time and space are the unobstructed outworking of his singular immutable decree. There is one simple cause, but an incomprehensible multitude of effects.

As creatures, then, we use the language of our affections, the motions of man's soul worked out through his body relative to good or evil, to give names to the temporal effects of God's decree. But distinctions must be made in order to safeguard the divine and human natures on either side of these analogical predications.

When God's actions are described in the language of affections, we must determine whether they describe a

---

[15] Leigh, *A Systeme or Body of Divinity*, 161.

perfection in God that infinitely surpasses a virtue in creatures, like love, joy, mercy, etc., or if they simply create a point of contact between a creaturely action and a divine action, like repentance, grief, vengeance, etc. For example, acknowledging that God loves and humans love does not equate their love. God does not have human love. For mankind, love is an affection, a disposition, a state of action or being, brought about by good or evil perceived in an external object (or ourselves). We will do many foolish things, innocent or otherwise, "in the name of love" because we are affected by the object of our love.

It is not so with God. God *is* love. His love is not an affection or a passion, a potential motion of a being with interrelating constitutive parts and faculties. Rather God's love is essential, unchangeable, and everlasting, a true consolation for his people.

Conclusion

In conclusion, without careful definitions we are too often poised on the precipices of false dilemmas, talking past each other. Does God have affections? Your answer depends on your approach. Does God have motions of the soul worked out through the body relative to good or evil? No, of course not. That is impossible. Affections are not necessarily *sinful*, but they are always *creaturely*. But, in the simple essence of God can we distinguish, notionally, certain perfections which bear the names of human affections, such as love, joy, mercy, justice, and more? And do we name God's actions in time and space according to how they reflect the fullness of his divine perfections? Absolutely. To deny affections of God often sounds like an extreme negation, perhaps indicating that in God there is no love, mercy, joy, etc. It seems to throw out the baby with the bathwater. But to deny affections and passions of God is clearly to remove the creaturely and sinful elements of affections from God, and thus to make his essential perfections and unobstructed actions shine forth all the brighter.

And as our view expands to include more of the pieces and tools necessary for understanding this issue, are we taking into account the creaturely half of the equation? What are the prerequisites for positing affections, properly defined, or emotions of God? Ultimately, one is forced to add something to the one true simple spiritual God, to the God who is what he is, something which possesses the passive power to undergo change, something that is not God. And what are we left with? A "god" who might become what he was not rather than the one true God whose very name is "I am that I am." Amen.

Confessional Scripture References:

- Therefore, as to the eating of food offered to idols, we know that "an idol has no real existence," and that "there is no God but one." 5 For although there may be so-called gods in heaven or on earth—as indeed there are many "gods" and many "lords" — 6 yet for us there is one God, the Father, from whom are all things and for whom we exist, and one Lord, Jesus Christ, through whom are all things and through whom we exist. (1 Cor. 8:4-6)
- Hear, O Israel: The LORD our God, the LORD is one. (Deut. 6:4)
- But the LORD is the true God; he is the living God and the everlasting King. At his wrath the earth quakes, and the nations cannot endure his indignation. (Jer. 10:10)
- Listen to me, O Jacob, and Israel, whom I called! I am he; I am the first, and I am the last. (Isa. 48:12)
- God said to Moses, "I AM WHO I AM." And he said, "Say this to the people of Israel, 'I AM has sent me to you.'" (Exod. 3:14)

- God is spirit, and those who worship him must worship in spirit and truth. (John 4:24)
- To the King of the ages, immortal, invisible, the only God, be honor and glory forever and ever. Amen. (1 Tim. 1:17)
- Therefore watch yourselves very carefully. Since you saw no form on the day that the Lord spoke to you at Horeb out of the midst of the fire, 16 beware lest you act corruptly by making a carved image for yourselves, in the form of any figure, (Deut. 4:15-16)
- For I the Lord do not change; therefore you, O children of Jacob, are not consumed. (Mal. 3:6)
- But will God indeed dwell on the earth? Behold, heaven and the highest heaven cannot contain you; how much less this house that I have built! (1 Kings 8:27)
- Am I a God at hand, declares the Lord, and not a God far away? 24 Can a man hide himself in secret places so that I cannot see him? declares the Lord. Do I not fill heaven and earth? declares the Lord. (Jer. 23:23-24)
- Before the mountains were brought forth, or ever you had formed the earth and the world, from everlasting to everlasting you are God. (Psalm 90:2)

Study Questions

1. What is God?

2. What do the names of God teach us about who and what God is?

3. How does the way of negation help us consider if God has passions?

4. How does the way of eminence help us consider if God has passions?

5. What would we have to change about God in order for him to have passions?

Chapter 4

Perfections and Incarnation

We have completed all of the necessary ground work to answer the question, does God have affections and passions? We have looked at the Scriptures to gather a method of interpretation. We have examined human nature in order to understand passions and affections in their natural context. And we have studied the divine nature in order to see whether or not passions or affections are compatible with who and what God is. Having laid a foundation, what we are going to do is to ask and answer the question, does God have affections and passions? Then we are going to look at the doctrine of Christ the Mediator, and we are going to see how carefully the Reformed orthodox guarded the distinction of the two natures of Jesus Christ. This will serve as a summary example of the differences between divine and human nature, and the ways in which they cannot mix or cross.

Does God have Affections and Passions?

1. God does not have passions or affections; he has perfections.

Why does God not have passions or affections? We have defined passions and affections as *motions of the soul worked out through the body relative to perceived good or evil*. God does not have a soul, a body, or the faculties that belong to them. He does not perceive or interpret anything. And he does not react to anything. He cannot be acted upon. He cannot be changed or become anything more or less than what he is. Rather, God is all that he is, a most pure Spirit. He is simple, essential, actual, and perfect.

Properly defined, then, God does not and cannot have passions or affections. Taken as equal to affections (which we have just defined) or as a subset of affections (affections gone bad), God cannot have passions. Affections may not be inherently sinful, but they are inherently *creaturely* and eminently inconsistent with "a most pure spirit." The *way of negation* prevents us from attributing passions to God. Rather, all of the actions of God that creatures perceive in time and space are the unobstructed outworking of his singular immutable decree. There is one simple cause, but an incomprehensible multitude of effects.

Now, as we brought out in the last chapter through the way of eminence, removing passions from God causes his perfections to shine forth. So that is where we will turn now.

As creatures, we use the language of our affections to give names to those things which God causes to be effected in time and space. We see God acting in certain ways, and we use the language of our affections and passions to describe his actions. But because we realize that we cannot contain God in our language, we recognize that what is in God is different from what is in us. Distinctions must be made in order to safeguard the divine and human natures on either side of these analogical predications. Here we repeat again that phrase from Thomas Adams, "They are *perfections* in him, what are *affections* in us."[1]

So let's talk about some of the divine perfections that are originally in God and poorly represented in creatures. We

---

[1] Adams, *Workes*, 258.

will see the principles and methods we have developed being applied specifically. We are going to cover three things that are perfections in God, but affections in us: love, mercy, and anger.

Love

Here is what Theodore Beza has to say about God's love.

> The love that is in God, is no *passion arising of some good that it apprehends*, but it is *the very simple essence of God*. . . . The cause of that love of his, is not in the creatures, as though they were such as could allure God to love them, but *it is rather in God, who of himself is good, and pours goodness upon his creatures.*[2]

Notice that Beza says that love *as a passion* is not in God. Love for us is when we perceive some good, and act towards it. That is an affection, according to every definition we have seen. And love is not so for God. He does not perceive or encounter good and fall in love. He is love. Love is doing good to another. God is good in himself, and causes good to others of his own goodness. Therefore God is love, essentially. He does not have love as humans know it. We love him, because he first loved us.

Now let's listen to Zanchius:

> That we may know whether that love do properly agree to God, we must first see what love is, and what it is to love. . . . For to love, in all men's judgment, is nothing else but to be carried with an affection of mind towards any thing in such sort, as that the mind and affection may rest in the enjoying

---

[2] Theodore Beza, *Propositions and Principles of Divinitie, Propovnded and Disputed in the Vniversitie of Geneva* (n.p., 1595), 22. Italics original.

of the same. . . . Hence is easily gathered what love is; namely, a passion of the mind, whereby we are so affected towards any man, as that forgetting ourselves, we are wholly carried towards him. . . . *But love in God is not such as it is in us,* no more than that being which he has imparted unto us is like to that which he is in himself. . . . *And it is in God most perfect* (for there is nothing imperfect in him) but in us imperfect, and joined with passion and impure affections and weakness of the mind. Wherefore although we be drawn through the consideration of that love which is in us, to consider what manner of love that of God is, *yet are not all things to be transferred to God's love which we do find in our own: but only those things which signify perfections,* and are most beseeming the nature of God. . . . Wherefore that rule which we have used elsewhere, is to be held, that whatsoever imperfection we find in our affections, love, and mercy, being purged as it were from all imperfection, is to be attributed to God. Therefore *love in God signifies no affection or passion, as in us, but altogether things perfect.*[3]

You can see the *via negationis* and the *via eminentiae* at work here. As we move from our love to God's love, we remove from it all imperfection, passion especially, and then we better declare the perfection of God.

Now let's hear from Wolfgang Musculus:

As touching men's affections which do go with the love of man, *it is not meet that we should refer them unto the nature of God in that sort as they be found in men.* In the nature of man, love believes all things, trusts all things, weeps with them which do weep, and is weak

---

[3] Zanchius, *Life euerlasting,* 357-58. Italics added.

with them which be weak, is it convenient, that the like be referred unto the love of God? The Scripture attributes many things unto God by figure and similitude of man's affections, which do not so agree unto the nature of God, as they do unto our nature. And yet for all that, it is not without reason, that it speaks unto men in this wise of God, to apply itself unto our capacity.[4]

Musculus reminds us not to equate man's love and God's love. But he also says that Scripture does not attribute love to God for no good reason. And as Beza and Zanchius have shown us, Scripture does so to tell us of God's perfection. God is love. And that is a perfection, not an affection. Let's move on to mercy. We will see the same principles applied.

Mercy

Musculus says again:

There be sundry causes whereupon the hearts of men be moved unto mercy. Now what the causes of Mercy be in God a man may safely enough search, so that he consider the Majesty of God, as it is most excellent, most just, and most happy. That one man has compassion upon another that is afflicted, it is no strange matter, for there is one self-same nature in both, one quality of nature, the like frailty, baseness, and general wretchedness of their whole life, and depravation, or crookedness of mind. But what has man in common with God? Nothing at all. He is most excellent, we most base: he most righteous, and we

---

[4] Wolfgang Musculus, *Common Places of Christian Religion*, trans. Iohn Man (London: Henry Bynnerman, 1578), 958-59. Italics added.

sinful: he happy in all respects, and we unhappy, and wretched in many respects. So that there is no cause of mercy in God, which can come of any communicating of nature, condition, life, and estate with us, whereas we do in all points beyond all measure vary from him. And yet for all that *he is so merciful*, that he delights also in mercy, more than in sacrifice. Therefore it remains, that *the greater the mercy is in God, than it is in the hearts of men, and the less that the causes of men's compassion do take place in him, the more manifest it is, that he has no other cause of his mercy, but his incomparable goodness of nature*, unto which we did also refer his lovingness towards man in the place before.[5]

We are merciful because we suffer and feel alongside of another person. We enter into their state and we pity them. We are overcome by sympathy or compassion. It is not so with God. But rather than making God uncaring, he is the one who helps the helpless though there is no reason in the helpless person for him to do so. We are moved to sympathy because we see something of ourselves in another person. We do not feel mercy for rocks being smashed because, well, who cares? If God is so different from us, couldn't he say the same? No, because the less God's mercy is conditioned upon his participation in our nature, the greater he is able to be merciful to all as he wills. Zanchius continues:

> . . . And this is the common opinion, which yet I do not simply approve.[6] For the reason why they think thus is, because *they consider mercy in us, and then transfer it from us unto God*: thinking that it is so

---

[5] Musculus, *Common Places*, 982-83. Italics added.

[6] Referring to the opinion of philosophers that mercy is not in God *in any sense* because mercy includes the idea of "heart misery" and "passion."

properly and of itself called mercy, as it is in us: and so for that it cannot be so in God, to wit, with passion, as it is in us. . . . But it is in my judgment far otherwise. For the name of *mercy, is first in God,* before it is in us; for it was in him first: and it is eternal in God. . . . For *God is merciful, of his own eternal and simple essence,* as also good, gentle, mighty: therefore that particle, *weakness of mind,* is not necessary in the definition of true mercy: but it is by accident that it is such in us: for that we are of such a nature as is subject to griefs and passions, so as we cannot hear, see, or think of another's misery, especially if he be of our affinity, or nation, or else joined unto us by the bond of nature, or friendship, without sympathy and grief. . . . Rather, as wisdom, life, justice, goodness, and other good gifts, so also mercy should first of itself and properly be said of God, and secondly and less properly of us: *for that is perfect in God, and imperfect in us.*[7]

We cannot go from human mercy to divine mercy. If you do, God cannot have mercy at all. But God is perfectly merciful. Mercy workers get overwhelmed. They see a lot of suffering and they sometimes have to stop or take breaks. Ministers in the ministry experience this. God is not subject to such weakness. He is like an immune doctor treating Ebola patients. That is the God I need and want, not the doctor who might get sick from me or with me. God's mercy is a perfection, not a passion or affection. Now on to God's anger.

Anger

Thomas Adams says:

---

[7] Zanchius, *Life everlasting,* 375-77. Italics added.

God may be *angry*, and sin is the cause of his anger; that's the first Proposition. Man may be angry without sin, not without perturbation: God is angry without either perturbation or sin. His anger is in his nature, not by anthropopathy, but properly; being his corrective Justice, or vindicative Justice. . . . Our anger is an impotent passion: His a most clear, free, and just operation. *By this affection in ourselves, we may guess at the perfection that is in God.*[8]

This is probably the best example of the problem of human language. Notice what Adams says. He is saying that God is angry, but how does he understand and define that? He defines it as an operation of justice. God will punish sin. Where there is sin, God will punish it. So, you cannot make God angry. God is not eternally burning with anger. Rather, we use the term angry to describe God's immutable justice. And whereas we get angry and cannot do anything about it, God perfectly brings judgment on the objects of his wrath.

It is very difficult to think about anger without passion. Adams even says that we can be angry and not sin, yet we cannot be angry without passion. But God's anger is his justice, a perfection, not an affection, a purposeful operation, not a passion.

2. Locating Scripture's connections

Now that you have seen all of the pieces of the argument in action, think back to some of the Scripture verses we covered in the first chapter. We looked at passages that describe God as regretting and repenting, and then Scripture says that God is not like a man and does not do such things. Rather, God does not change and always accomplishes what he

---

[8] Thomas Adams, *God's Anger and Man's Comfort* (London: Tho. Maxey, 1653), 6. Italics added.

purposes to do. So then, as you read the Scriptures, you need to make sure that you use the way of eminence and the way of negation. And when Scripture describes God in the language of human emotions, or human passions and affections, ask yourself if the connection is between a divine perfection poorly shadowed in humans, as when God is said to be loving, merciful, or angry, or if Scripture is connecting an *action* of God with a human action, as when God is said to be grieved in his heart, to repent, or to regret.

I trust that the examples of love, mercy, and anger are sufficient to show how we can see God described in human emotional language while understanding those things as perfections. But let me give you a few more helpful quotes to reinforce the point.

Scripture's connection in a divine perfection

Here are two quotes that I hope will help. John Preston said:

> If God should have *love* in him, or *justice*, or *wisdom*, or *life*, or any other quality different from his essence, *as the creatures have them*, he should be what he is, not originally of himself, but derivatively, and by participation, and so imperfectly: as to be fired is more imperfect than to be fire it self, to be gilded is more imperfect than to be gold it self.[9]

John Arrowsmith said:

> The mercy of God springs from within, and has no original cause without himself. Human affection is commonly both begotten and fed by somewhat without, in the thing or person beloved; as culinary

---

[9] John Preston, *Life Eternall Or, A Treatise of the Knowledge of the Divine Essence and Attributes* (London: R.B., 1631), 49. Italics added.

fire must be kindled and kept in by external materials: But God loves because he loves, and shows mercy on whom he will show mercy; as celestial fire is fuel to itself.[10]

Scripture's connection in a corresponding action

When you read in the Scriptures that God repented, or relented, or took vengeance, or was provoked to wrath, or was grieved in his heart, you have to remove the passion of those statements, and connect them to an action. Not everything is in God in a greater and essential measure. For example, to repent or relent is to stop doing what you were doing, and start doing something else. We experience this with grief of mind as we are confronted by unforeseen circumstances. God, however, decrees to begin a work, and to undo, and to begin a different work. There is no change in God.

When God is provoked to wrath or takes vengeance, it is not because he was awoken from a state of slumber into a state of rage. Remove the passion. God is perfectly just, thus whenever he chooses to pour out his judgment, which he often holds back for a time, it can be said that he took vengeance.

When God removes from our hearts that comfort of his presence that we desire, has he departed from us or stopped being loving?[11] No, he has brought about a change in us in order to accomplish a higher purpose.

---

[10] John Arrowsmith, *Armilla Catechetica. A Chain of Principles* (Cambridge: John Field, 1659), 160.

[11] See the Confession of Faith (17.1): "The sensible sight of the light of God, may for a time be clouded . . . yet he is still the same."

When he is grieved in his heart, does God suffer pain or experience heartbreak? Of course not,[12] but if mankind's wickedness was greater than we have ever seen it and if God is perfectly just, could not his action against their wickedness be described in the language of heartbroken repentance and vengeance in order to describe the intensity of the sin and the retribution? Zanchius concludes this point.

> The affections which are attributed unto God are, rejoicing, and sorrow in the heart of God, anger, zeal, jealousy, hatred, and repentance. And these are not motions and perturbations in God, as they are in men: for he is free from all change & perturbation, and always the same: but they are works or actions of God, which in some sort are like to the actions of men, which arise from these affections.[13]

Does God have passions and affections? No. He has perfections.

The Doctrine of Christ the Mediator

Now we are going to do a flyby of the doctrine of Christ the Mediator. What we want to note is that orthodox Christianity has always confessed that the Mediator Jesus Christ is one person with two natures. This is often referred to as the hypostatic union. In the one person, there are united two natures.

---

[12] And remember that if he did, his grief would be essential, eternal, and infinite.

[13] Zanchius, *Life everlasting*, 659-60.

1. The divine and human natures and the unity of the person (hypostatic union)

Let's look at the Confession of Faith, chapter 8, "Of Christ the Mediator," paragraph 2.

> The Son of God, the second person in the Holy Trinity, being very and eternal God, the brightness of the Father's glory, of one substance and equal with him who made the world . . . did . . . take upon him man's nature, with all the essential properties and common infirmities thereof, yet without sin . . . so that two whole, perfect, and distinct natures were inseparably joined together in one person, without conversion, composition, or confusion; which person is very God and very man, yet one Christ, the only mediator between God and man.

The Son of God, the second person of the Holy Trinity, is of one substance with the Father and the Spirit. He is truly God. Everything that is true of God is true of God the Son. We worship one God in three persons. God is impassible. Thus, God the Son is impassible. He has no passions or affections, but only perfections.

Let's hear Zanchius on this. He says:

> We therefore acknowledge and confess . . . that in Christ there is one only Person, and that eternal, most simple and most perfect, and remaining the same forever, to wit, the Person of the eternal Son of God; and, that unto this eternal Person there was added in time, not another person, but another nature, that is, the human; but yet not as a part of that Person, by which it was assumed, but a thing far different from it, and yet assumed into the unity thereof. And further in the third place, we confess

that in one and the same Person of Christ there are now two natures: the divine and human. . . . Wherefore we are not afraid to say, that Christ now consists of the divine & human nature being assumed into the unity of person.[14]

Now, the two natures in the unity of the person becomes the basis for what is called the communication of properties, or the *communicatio idiomatum*.

2. The communication of properties (*communicatio idiomatum*)

The *communicatio idiomatum* is the realization that as the one person acts, as Jesus Christ acts, he does so according to each nature. And each nature is separate, the divine never becoming the human, and the human never becoming the divine. We confess this in chapter 8, paragraph 7.

> Christ, in the work of mediation, acts according to both natures, by each nature doing that which is proper to itself; yet by reason of the unity of the person, that which is proper to one nature is sometimes in Scripture, attributed to the person denominated by the other nature.

In paragraph four of the same chapter of the Confession, we see an example of this in play. Jesus endured sorrows in in his soul, and sufferings in his body. What are the body and soul? They are the parts of a human nature. Jesus' grief and suffering were not sustained in the divine nature. "This office the Lord Jesus did most willingly undertake . . .

---

[14] Girolamo Zanchius, *The Whole Body of Christian Religion*, trans. D. Ralph Winterton (London: John Redmayne, 1659), 86-87.

enduring most grievous *sorrows in his soul,* and most painful *sufferings in his body"* (8.4. italics added).

John Flavel reinforces the point. He said:

> Hence, in the last place, follows, as another excellent fruit of this Union, *The concourse and co-operation of each Nature to his Mediatory Works: For in them he acts according to both Natures.* The human Nature doing what is Human, *viz.* Suffering, Sweating, Bleeding, Dying: and his Divine Nature stamping all these with infinite value; and so both sweetly concur unto one glorious work and design of Mediation.[15]

And Nehemiah Coxe said:

> The Scriptures say indeed, that the Prince of Life was killed, and the Lord of Glory was crucified: So the Scripture says also, that God purchased his church by his blood; and laid down his life for us: The person that died was very God, the Prince of Life and Lord of Glory, but it was in the human nature, and not in his divine that he suffered, although both made but one person; and to reject this, and say . . . that as God *etc.* his Blood was shed, he was crucified and died, *i.e.* that all these things befell the Divine as well as the Human nature; is impious to that degree, as may make a tender heart bleed, and the ears of a godly man to tingle.[16]

---

15 John Flavel, *The Fountain of Life Opened: Or, A Display of Christ* (London: Thomas Parkhurst, 1698), 48-49.

16 Nehemiah Coxe, *Vindiciae Veritatis, Or a Confutation of the Heresies and Gross Errors of Thomas Collier,* (London: Nath. Ponder, 1677), 17.

Think about this. If God can sustain suffering in his divine nature, why was the incarnation necessary? Why did the Son of God take on our flesh, if God could sustain suffering as God? God is not man. Man is not God. But the beauty of the gospel is the God-man, Jesus Christ. He is Immanuel, God with us. And his sufferings and temptation were real. He endured all of that without sin. But all of his obedience was real as well. He was and is a perfect man. You see, divine impassibility not only causes God's essential perfections to shine forth, but also, as we recognize the distinction of the natures in the one person Jesus Christ, it should cause us to praise our Redeemer. It should cause us to praise our Savior. And he is worthy. He is man. But he is God.

Find consolation in these truths. The writer to the Hebrews sums it all up in an amazing statement of comfort. He says:

> Since then we have a great high priest who has passed through the heavens, Jesus, the Son of God, let us hold fast our confession. 15 For we do not have a high priest who is unable to sympathize with our weaknesses, but one who in every respect has been tempted as we are, yet without sin. 16 Let us then with confidence draw near to the throne of grace, that we may receive mercy and find grace to help in time of need. (Heb. 4:14-16)

Conclusion

Does God have passions and affections? No. He has perfections. Does Jesus have two natures in the unity of the one person, and does he act according to each nature? Yes. Does that mean that we have a perfect Mediator?

Absolutely. And he is worthy of our praise. The way to the throne of grace is wide open because of him. You are praying to a man who is God. He knows your weakness. He is like us, yet without sin. Paul and Barnabas told the crowds, "We are men of like passions with you." James told his readers that Elijah was a man with passions like us. But Jesus is like us and unlike us. He suffered, truly, but perfectly. His passion was not involuntary, rather he set his face like a flint and went to the cross willingly, in his human nature. He stared torture and death in the face, and obeyed. He went like a lamb to the slaughter. Praise Father, Son, and Holy Ghost. Amen.

Study Questions

1. Does God have passions?

2. What is the difference between God's love, mercy, and anger and our love, mercy, and anger?

3. What do Scripture passages that describe God in the language of affections and passions communicate to us?

4. Did God the Son suffer or undergo any change in his divine nature as a result of the incarnation?

5. If Christ the Mediator has two natures, does each nature perform the same actions equally?

Chapter 5

Personal Applications and Pastoral Implications

Thus far we have covered the exegetical foundations and the rules of interpretation that they gave us. We have also covered the human nature and how passions and affections are a part of it. In the third chapter we covered the divine nature and why God cannot have affections or passions, but rather he has perfections. And in the previous chapter we talked about God's perfections as well as how the incarnation demonstrates the points we had covered because in the incarnation we have a divine nature and a human nature united in one person, but never mixing. The incarnation occurred "without conversion, composition, or confusion," as our Confession of Faith says.[1]

In this chapter we will cover the personal applications and pastoral implications of divine impassibility. Some have said that this doctrine is simply an abstract theoretical exercise in speculative theology and that it has no real practical or pastoral connections with reality. I would beg to differ, and I trust that by the end of this chapter you will see the wonderful benefit that comes from knowing the perfections of the God we worship.

But before we jump into this, let me give you three general reasons why impassibility is practical. First, the

---

[1] 2LCF 8.2.

doctrine of God is practical. When God sent Moses to Israel, Moses replied that the people would want to know the God that was rescuing them. God revealed himself as "I am that I am." That is important. If you have a relationship with someone, then knowing who they are is very practical. So then, the doctrine of God is practical.

Second, the doctrine of God is central. It is a hub out of which the rest of the areas of theology flow. Think about the Confession of Faith. What follows from the doctrine of God? The decree, providence, creation, man's fall, sin, and man's salvation through Jesus Christ, and on and on. Are those chapters profoundly affected by who God is? Of course they are. They largely describe his actions. And even on a surface level, once you define the parameters of who God is, you then take all of that with you every time you mention his name. And looking beyond systematic theology, when we sing hymns of praise or say, "Dear God," in our prayers, what is the content of the name "God"? To what are we referring? You see, the doctrine of God is not just practical, it is also central.

Third, the doctrine of God is biblical. What I mean is that when you read in the Scriptures that God was grieved in his heart or provoked to wrath or that he repented or that he changed his mind, you need to know whether or not those phrases describe God in his divine nature or if they use human language to communicate certain truths to us, but not in a one-to-one connection. It is biblical, and we are Bible-readers. So it is practical in general for at least those three reasons.

The Personal Applications of Divine Impassibility

I once had a dream that I was on top of the tallest building in Los Angeles. It was very windy, and I could barely stand up or catch my balance. While the view was incredible, it was very scary to be in such a vulnerable and unstable position. I wanted to get inside, to go down the stairs or elevator, and to get out. I did not feel safe. I felt unsafe because I did not have a firm foundation. I felt like the building itself was moving in the wind, not just me.

Everything depends on its foundation. If you are on a bridge, you are trusting the concrete or wood under your feet. And you are trusting the support columns beneath the top layer. And you are trusting the ground that those columns have been sunk into. If you built a large, heavy, strong bridge in a swamp without getting down to a firm foundation, the top-heavy strength would only make it sink faster. If you built a giant bridge with enormous strength and airlifted it over the ocean and dropped it into the ocean, would the bridge be safe to cross? No, it would sink to the bottom of the ocean. Its supports would not be deep enough.

So then, what we need in our times of trials and difficulties is a foundation so foundational that there is nothing in heaven or earth, past, present, or future that can move, remove, or shake it. When you are in the darkness of doubts and in the depths of distress, what is it that you need to remember? Where does the Bible take us in our times of discouragement and despair? I want to give you two points at the same time to show the personal applications of divine impassibility: first, *God's unchanging perfections are the foundation of his promises* and second, *God's unchanging perfections are the foundation of your perseverance*. We are going to cover both of these points together.

Look at Exodus 3:13-15 with me. Think about Moses' situation in this narrative. Israel was so thoroughly oppressed and suppressed by the Egyptians that the Egyptians could kill all of their male children, and Israel could not stop them. Can you imagine a more complete state of subjugation and control than the fact that all of your male children are being murdered? How in the world can Moses

take a message to those people and expect them to believe
that a God can deliver them? Read verses 13-15 with me.
This passage says:

> Then Moses said to God, "If I come to the people of
> Israel and say to them, 'The God of your fathers has
> sent me to you,' and they ask me, 'What is his name?'
> what shall I say to them?" 14 God said to Moses, "I
> AM WHO I AM." And he said, "Say this to the
> people of Israel, 'I AM has sent me to you.'" 15 God
> also said to Moses, "Say this to the people of Israel,
> 'The LORD, the God of your fathers, the God of
> Abraham, the God of Isaac, and the God of Jacob, has
> sent me to you.' This is my name forever, and thus I
> am to be remembered throughout all generations."
> (Exod. 3:13-15)

"I am who I am" has sent Moses to Israel. This name
says to Israel, "the God who is of himself, who stands on no
other, who comes from no other, and who is who he is, he
will deliver you." Who God is, the perfection of his
character, makes his promises and his word a sure and firm
foundation for the Israelites to trust in and upon which to
stand and persevere. Who God is, is the foundation of his
promises and Israel's perseverance.

Consider Malachi 3:6 with me. "For I the LORD do not
change; therefore you, O children of Jacob, are not
consumed." Think about this statement. It has two simple
parts. It has a statement, and then a conclusion that follows
from that statement. The statement is "I the LORD do not
change." The conclusion? "Therefore you, O children of
Jacob, are not consumed." God's love is not an affection or a
passion. God cannot be moved from not loving to loving. He
is love. And because he does not change, therefore you are
not consumed. The unchanging nature of God's love, God's
impassibility, is not simply an idea to be written about and

debated by scholars and theologians. It is the very reason that you and I wake up each morning and we say to ourselves, "My sins are forgiven." Because he does not change, therefore I am not consumed.

When God promises us in the new covenant that he will remember our sins no more, that he will cover our transgressions, he means it. When you forgive your spouse or someone else, it is likely that you mean it, and that their sin toward you fades from memory quite a bit. But down the road, if the person repeats the offense or does something similar, depending on your emotional, mental, and physical state, you may drag up their past sins and parade them before the person. In other words, whatever your intentions and feelings may have been at one point in time, they can change drastically at another. Your love can be provoked, and it can be suppressed. We grow in our relationships as we learn to forgive and love, but even the strongest relationships have had to go through this process of growth and learning. If we enjoy a loving, trusting relationship, surely it has been cultivated and promoted, and rightly so.

But with God, we are not dealing with a human being. We are not dealing with a creature. We are dealing with "I am who I am." And because he does not change, therefore we are not consumed. When he declares to us that our sins are forgiven and forgotten, they are indeed. And no sinfulness on our part will cause God to have an emotional reaction against us in the future.

We can sincerely say with Jeremiah the weeping prophet in Lamentations 3:21-24,

> But this I call to mind, and therefore I have hope: 22 The steadfast love of the LORD never ceases; his mercies never come to an end; 23 they are new every morning; great is your faithfulness. 24 "The LORD is my portion," says my soul, "therefore I will hope in him."

How do the biblical writers escape their lamentations and cries for help? How do they resolve their doubts and find stable ground upon which to stand in the tossing seas of life? They go to God and his unchanging nature.

Think about Psalm 73. This is a well-known Psalm in which the psalmist envies the wicked and cannot understand why they prosper in their wickedness while he languishes, bearing the name of Jehovah, apparently in vain. When he comes around in his thinking, what does he say?

> I was brutish and ignorant; I was like a beast toward you. 23 Nevertheless, I am continually with you; you hold my right hand. 24 You guide me with your counsel, and afterward you will receive me to glory. 25 Whom have I in heaven but you? And there is nothing on earth that I desire besides you. 26 My flesh and my heart may fail, but God is the strength of my heart and my portion forever. (Psalm 73:22-26)

The psalmist turns to the unchanging faithfulness of God as his anchor and mainstay.

This makes John's words all the sweeter when he says in 1 John 4:16, "So we have come to know and to believe the love that God has for us. God is love, and whoever abides in love abides in God, and God abides in him."

Impassibility refers to far more than just God's love. But God's love tends to be the perfect example of why this doctrine is so practical. While some people see it as denying real love to God, it simply shows that love in God is a perfection, while in us it is a passion or affection. And this, dear reader, is that foundation of all foundations that we need.

Let's read a few quotes from our Reformed forefathers that will drive the point home. John Preston said:

If *God* be such a *simple, first, pure,* and *absolute* being, then hence you may see, what a stable foundation our faith has to rest upon; we are built upon the lowest foundation in all the world, that is, upon the first, most absolute, and *simple,* and *pure,* and *entire* being; which I say is the lowest foundation, that depends upon no other, but all upon it: and this is the happy condition of all Christians, and of them alone.[2]

Edward Leigh said:

The Attributes of God are everlasting, constant and unchangeable, forever in him, at one time as well as another. . . . This may minister comfort to God's people; God's attributes are not mutable accidents, but his very essence: His love and mercy are like himself, infinite, immutable and eternal.[3]

Wolfgang Musculus said:

We do oftentimes perceive how inconstant and changeable any manner of good disposition of man's heart is. If you ask me the reason, it may be answered, that it is therefore unstable, because it is not naturally grafted in us, but bred by occasion, and changeable causes: so that when the cause ceases, the effect also ceases. The like cannot be thought of the goodness of God. For God is good, not upon occasion or upon causes given by any other thing, but naturally of himself, and therefore look how unchangeable he and his nature is, and so unchangeable in his goodness also.[4]

---

[2] Preston, *Life Eternall,* 51. Italics original.
[3] Leigh, *A Systeme or Body of Divinity,* 161.
[4] Musculus, *Common Places,* 952-53.

Personal Applications and Pastoral Implications

Benedict Pictet said:

From the *simplicity* of God follows his *immutability,* which denotes nothing else than such a state of the divine essence and attributes, as is not subject to any change. Now this immutability is proved by scripture, "God is not a man, that he should lie; neither the son of man, that he should repent." (Numb. 23:19) "I am the Lord, I change not." (Mal. 3:6) "With whom is no variableness, neither shadow of turning." (James 1:17) Besides, that which possesses all perfection, cannot be changed. If God changed, he would do so either *for the better,* or *for the worse,* or *for something equal.* Now he cannot change *for the better,* because he is the best; neither *for the worse,* for then he would not possess all perfections. . . . Therefore, there is no changeableness in God . . . not in his *essence,* for being the *first,* he cannot be superseded by any prior being; being *all-powerful;* he cannot be injured by any; being most *simple,* he can be corrupted by none; being *immense,* he cannot be increased or lessened; being *eternal,* he cannot fail. There is no change in his *eternity,* for where there is no succession, there is no mutation; neither in his *understanding,* for the knowledge of God is all-perfect; nor in his *will,* for the will of God is all-wise, to which nothing unforeseen can happen, so as to compel him to change his intentions for the better. Again, nothing can prevent and resist his will; he does, indeed, will the various changes of things, but his will itself remains unchangeable. This immutability of God is the foundation of our faith and hope.[5]

---

[5] Benedict Pictet, *Christian Theology,* trans. Frederick Reyroux (London: R.B. Seeley and W. Burnside, 1834), 99-100. Italics original.

If that is not practical, I do not know what is.

Let's conclude this section with one more passage of Scripture. The psalmist, in Psalm 77:6-13, says:

> I said, "Let me remember my song in the night; let me meditate in my heart." Then my spirit made a diligent search: 7 "Will the Lord spurn forever, and never again be favorable? 8 Has his steadfast love forever ceased? Are his promises at an end for all time? 9 Has God forgotten to be gracious? Has he in anger shut up his compassion?" Selah 10 Then I said, "I will appeal to this, to the years of the right hand of the Most High." 11 I will remember the deeds of the LORD; yes, I will remember your wonders of old. 12 I will ponder all your work, and meditate on your mighty deeds. 13 Your way, O God, is holy. What god is great like our God?

When you are in the midst of affliction, discouraged, distressed, and distraught, you need a firm foundation. How can you persevere in difficulty? You trust in God who loves you unchangeably. And when we begin to question how the difficult circumstances in which we find ourselves can be the product of God who is love, we must remember that God brings good out of evil. We must look to the cross of Jesus Christ where his love is displayed most clearly and definitively.

Our confidence is not in a promise that life will always get better, but rather that when life ends, it has only just begun. In other words, our confidence is not in this earthly body or any earthly pleasures here and now, but rather new life, eternal life, and new creation. And if that is our perspective, then trials and afflictions become means of teaching us to look to eternity and our future hope rather than our present difficulties. And it means that we can persevere through the most difficult times because even if they become the worst possible, we know that our unchanging God who loves us will not fail to deliver us from eternal damnation and judgment.

Think about the twenty-one Coptic Christians who were murdered by ISIS. Can it get any worse for them here on earth? They were in captivity, tied up, and brutally murdered at the hands of enemies. Can it get any worse, humanly speaking? Surely it cannot. Is God unchangeably loving, good, and wise in such a situation? Surely he is. Their deaths are a new beginning, not a judgment or curse. They are at home with the Lord Jesus (2 Cor. 5:8). And their testimony of faithfulness unto death is the very message that their killers mocked. In the very act of murdering those believers, their enemies were only proclaiming their message even louder.

When you go to bed and when you wake up, when you enter the hospital and when you come home, when you are born and when you die, from start to finish, any time and at all times, your God is the God who is love, who is mercy, who is kindness, who is justice, who is goodness, who is wisdom, and who is holiness.

When you are in need of a foundation upon which to persevere, remember, "I the LORD do not change. Therefore you, O believer, are not consumed." Recall this to mind, and have hope. The steadfast love of the Lord never ceases; his mercies never come to an end. They are new every morning. Great is his faithfulness. The Lord is your portion, says your soul, therefore hope in him. Thomas Manton said:

> It is the folly of the children of God, to question his love, because of the greatness of their afflictions, as if their interest did change with their condition, and

God were not the God of the Vallies, as well as the
God of the hills.[6]

God has many purposes in his actions. As his children,
we must trust him and persevere. But we have such a
foundation in which to trust and upon which to persevere.
Whether you are in a valley or a hill, your God is "I am who
I am." He is Jehovah, the one who does not change. And he
is love. Trust in his perfections and promises, and persevere
by his grace and in his power.

The Pastoral Implications
of Divine Impassibility

I am calling the following assertions "pastoral implications"
because they profoundly affect the way that pastors operate
in the church. The way that we comfort and counsel
Christians is greatly affected by this. And especially, the way
that we preach the gospel is affected by this. The doctrine of
God is a hub for theology. It should not surprise us, then,
that divine impassibility has direct implications for the
preaching of the gospel and all areas of pastoral life. Let's
work through a few considerations here.

1. Without any doubt or deviation, God will punish the wicked and vindicate the righteous.

Why do we preach the gospel? Or put another way, why is it
necessary to preach the gospel? Chapter 20 of the Confession

---

[6] Thomas Manton, *A Second Volume of Sermons, Sermons Upon the
Seventeenth Chapter of St. John, Sermon I* (London: J. Astwood, 1684), 7. The
pagination resets in each section of this volume.

of Faith reminds us that the preaching of the gospel is necessary because of man's fall into sin, the breaking of the covenant of works. We preach the gospel to the world because they are sinners in need of salvation, in need of forgiveness. But an important part of the gospel message is to declare to the world that it is sinful. Mankind in Adam and in our own lives has disobeyed God's laws.

Now, God is immutably and perfectly just. He does not subscribe to a system of justice. Rather he is justice. Justice is what God says it is. So, when we tell someone that they are a sinner, it means that there is a serious problem between them and God. They have sinned against God almighty. And they must answer to God's justice, or we could say, God himself.

But is God like a god of Greek mythology? Is he like a Mob Boss or a dictator that someone annoyed? Is his justice simply a whim? Are we telling sinners that there is someone they need to pay off? Are we telling them that they have offended someone and they just need to smooth things out? Certainly not. We are telling them that *without any doubt and any deviation, God will punish the wicked*. He will punish sinners. And we can tell them with all conviction and sobriety that so long as you remain a sinner, you have every assurance that at the final judgment you will be sent to everlasting judgment for your sins.

If God is impassible, then he cannot be provoked or swayed or moved. Preaching the gospel with an impassible God behind the threat of judgment gives it all of its power and force. Stephen Charnock said:

> The will of God is unchangeably set to love righteousness and hate iniquity, and from this hatred to punish it; and if a righteous creature contracts the wrath of God, or a sinful creature has the communications of God's love, it must be by a change in themselves. Is the sun changed when it

hardens one thing and softens another, according to the disposition of the several subjects? Or when the sun makes a flower more fragrant, and a dead carcass more noisome[7]? There are divers effects, but the reason of that diversity is not in the sun, but in the subject; the sun is the same, and produces those different effects by the same quality of heat; so if an unholy soul approach to God, God looks angrily upon him; if a holy soul come before him, the same immutable perfection in God draws out his kindness towards him.[8]

Think about what he is saying. God is unchanging. The same perfection in God that punishes wickedness also loves righteousness. When you put butter in the sun, or refried beans, two different things happen. Butter melts, and refried beans dry up. Does putting butter in the sun change the sun? Does putting refried beans in the sun change the sun? No, but the sun changes each one in different ways. One is melted; the other dries up.

So also, we can and must assure sinful mankind that so long as they approach God as a sinner, they will encounter his absolute and immutable justice. We call his justice "wrath" or "anger" not because God is an overheating human, but rather so that everyone understands the danger and threat. Unless we are changed, we will be judged as sinners. The law admits of no leniency. It condemns all.

This is biblical. Paul says in Romans 3:19-20,

Now we know that whatever the law says it speaks to those who are under the law, so that every mouth may be stopped, and the whole world may be held accountable to God. [20] For by works of the law no

---

[7] Foul-smelling.
[8] Charnock, *Works*, 1:227-28.

Personal Applications and Pastoral Implications

human being will be justified in his sight, since through the law comes knowledge of sin.

The fact that the law condemns all is universally true because all are fallen in Adam. But if there were a righteous person, the law would vindicate that person. In other words, if you took that righteous person to court, *the same law* would vindicate their name and say, "innocent." Paul also said in Romans 2:13-15,

> For it is not the hearers of the law who are righteous before God, but the doers of the law who will be justified. 14 For when Gentiles, who do not have the law, by nature do what the law requires, they are a law to themselves, even though they do not have the law. 15 They show that the work of the law is written on their hearts, while their conscience also bears witness, and their conflicting thoughts accuse or even excuse them.

Everyone knows, by nature, that there are right things and wrong things, good and bad. In other words, we have a natural knowledge of God's law. And though we are sinners and cannot do anything to gain God's favor, we know that he would approve our good works *if* we could perform them. We know that God punishes wickedness and vindicates righteousness.

But we must assert along with this knowledge of right and wrong, that God does these things immutably and perfectly and absolutely. He is not a judge that can be swayed to pity if you are guilty. He is not a judge who can be swayed to vengeance if you are innocent. God's justice will perfectly distribute judgment to the wicked, and vindication to the righteous. And every sinner must see himself in this light, as a guilty, condemned traitor on trial for sins against God himself.

This should of course raise the question, if God cannot be moved to pity towards the guilty, then what hope does anyone have of escaping his justice and judgment? The answer is that while God does not change, we can change in relation to his justice. But if we cannot change ourselves, what can be done? What is the solution? And the answer of course lies in the mediation of Jesus Christ, his incarnation and atonement. This brings us to our second consideration.

2. Without any doubt or deviation, God will justify all those who trust in Jesus Christ.

If any sinner is to become righteous, then he must be purged of his sinful record and given a new standing in righteousness. John 3:16-18 says:

> For God so loved the world, that he gave his only Son, that whoever believes in him should not perish but have eternal life. 17 For God did not send his Son into the world to condemn the world, but in order that the world might be saved through him. 18 Whoever believes in him is not condemned, but whoever does not believe is condemned already, because he has not believed in the name of the only Son of God.

God did not have to be persuaded or moved to kindness and mercy. He is kindness and mercy. And he, of his own will, chose some to receive eternal life, leaving others in their trespasses and sins. And for those who are elected, the work of God the Son is applied to their account. His sufferings erase their condemnation. And his obedience clothes them in robes of righteousness. And the same perfection of justice that condemns the wicked now justifies the believer. But what makes the believer's salvation or justification so certain and stable is the fact that it is rooted and grounded upon Jesus' perfect sinless obedience. And God vindicates the righteous. God cannot and will not punish the righteous because that would be a self-contradiction of his own character. Rather, God punished Jesus for our sins, and by his stripes we are made whole.

This foundation allows us to approach the truly hopeless and helpless sinner, condemned and awaiting eternal punishment, and to say to him or her, "Without any doubt or deviation, if you go to God in and through Jesus Christ, you will be saved. You will be justified!" And this is biblical. Romans 10:9-13 says:

> because, if you confess with your mouth that Jesus is Lord and believe in your heart that God raised him from the dead, you will be saved. 10 For with the heart one believes and is justified, and with the mouth one confesses and is saved. 11 For the Scripture says, 'Everyone who believes in him will not be put to shame.' 12 For there is no distinction between Jew and Greek; for the same Lord is Lord of all, bestowing his riches on all who call on him. 13 For 'everyone who calls on the name of the Lord will be saved.'

John declares this in some of my favorite verses in all of the Bible.

> And this is the testimony, that God gave us eternal life, and this life is in his Son. 12 Whoever has the Son has life; whoever does not have the Son of God does not have life. 13 I write these things to you who believe in the name of the Son of God that you may know that you have eternal life. (1 John 5:11-13)

In pastoral counseling, or fellowship one with another, we can say to each other that no matter what afflictions God permits in my life, and no matter how sinful I am, God's love towards me in Christ does not change. God does not have bad days. He does not have mood swings. He does not get annoyed. He does not change. Surely as a Father, God can cause me to feel separated from him, and he can chastise me in a number of ways, yet he does not cease to love me, nor is the status of my justification in Jesus Christ ever called into question. Without any doubt or deviation, God will justify all those who trust in Jesus Christ.

In light of these things, if God is chastising you, and permitting affliction in your life, it is not because he has changed, but because he is changing you. God is unchangeably good, wise, and loving. And because of this, when you are in affliction and trials you should not think that God is angry with you and doing mean things to you. Rather, you should ask yourself, "What lessons is God teaching me, and how should I be changed by this affliction?" If he is a loving Father, and indeed he is, his purpose is not to condemn but to chastise, not to punish but to teach, train, and discipline.

At the root of this is the truth that God does not change. He does not have passions or affections, but perfections. And God's perfection of justice punishes the wicked and vindicates the righteous. We, being righteous in and through Jesus Christ, are justified. God's law and justice vindicate us; they declare us innocent and righteous. And that is the gospel. Everyone who calls on the name of the Lord will be saved. No one who goes to him will be cast out or put to shame.

If God has passions or affections, how can we preach the gospel? Think about this with me. How can we declare the certainty of God's judgment or the certainty of his salvation if God has emotions like we do, or has states of being like we do, or can be moved from one disposition to another like we are? What will root and ground our statements about God? There would have to be some higher grounding cause for trusting God's threats and promises than his character and being. In which case, God would not be God. And we have already mentioned in another chapter that if God has passions and affections, and if he can sustain in his being the experiences that we have, then why was it even necessary for God the Son to take on our flesh? He could have suffered as God.

You see, the very foundations of the Christian gospel message can easily be dug up, quite by accident, when we are not careful with theology. Yet, when we read the Scriptures carefully, and listen to the collective wisdom of the past, we find a firm foundation for the Christian faith and the preaching of the law and the gospel, God's unchanging character and impassibility. He will punish the wicked. He will vindicate the righteous. And he will justify all those who trust in Jesus Christ, without doubt and without deviation. This leads us to our third and final consideration.

3. Without any doubt or deviation, God will keep his promises.

Think about the Lord's Supper with me. A sacrament is a visible word. It is a symbol for something else. It tells us something. It has a message. What is the message of the Lord's Supper? What do the bread and wine tell us? They are visible promises. They are a testimony that Christ's sacrifice, once offered, is the promise of our forgiveness of sins. They are the promises of the new covenant. The bread and wine are symbols of God's unchanging promises to his people in Christ. They are symbols of God's unchanging love to his people in Christ. They are a collective confession of the church of Jesus Christ that he has died and he will return. We proclaim his death only until he comes.

This is the very identity and unique message of Christianity. And we proclaim it with the confidence that without any doubt or deviation, God will keep his promises. And we know that his promises are certain to us because they come from an immutable and impassible God.

We could pile verse upon verse here showing the unchanging promises of God to us in and through Christ in the new covenant. But remember with me that God the Father has made promises to God the Son in the covenant of redemption. The certainty of the new covenant is not only grounded in the person and work of Christ, but also in the covenant that stands behind it, the covenant of redemption.

Consider Hebrews 7:18-26 with me. The author, referring to the Levitical priesthood, says:

> For on the one hand, a former commandment is set aside because of its weakness and uselessness 19 (for the law made nothing perfect); but on the other hand, a better hope is introduced, through which we draw near to God. 20 *And it was not without an oath.* For those who formerly became priests were made such without an oath, 21 but this one was made a priest *with an oath* by the one who said to him: *"The Lord has sworn and will not change his mind, 'You are a priest forever.'"* 22 This makes Jesus the guarantor of a better covenant. 23 The former priests were many in number, because they were prevented by death from continuing in office, 24 but he holds his priesthood permanently, because he continues forever. 25 Consequently, he is able to save to the uttermost those who draw near to God through him, since he always lives to make intercession for them. 26 For it was indeed fitting that we should have such a high priest, holy, innocent, unstained, separated from

sinners, and exalted above the heavens. (emphasis added)

The Mediator, Jesus Christ, is better than the Levites not only because he cannot die, and not just because he lives forever, but there is more. God the Father swore to him, *and will not change his mind.* You know what you call someone who does all that they will and whose mind cannot be changed? You call them immutable and impassible. Jesus Christ's priesthood on our behalf, his role as Mediator of the new covenant, is grounded by the oath of God the Father that he should be a priest forever.

Let me remind you of why this is so wonderful for us. Nicholas Mosley describes our nature and says:

> It is not in our own power whether we will be stirred with Affections or no; It is as possible to prevent them all as to go out of ourselves, or to give ourselves a new nature; no more than we can refuse to wink with the eye when a sudden blow is offered at it, or refuse to yawn when we see a yawning sleepy fellow.[9]

With that in mind, let us be reminded of how marvelous our God is by contrast. Edward Leigh sums up the arguments we have been making and drives the point home. He says:

> God is not changed any way, though he change his actions according to his good pleasure. First, this is terrible to wicked men, God is unchangeable, which has threatened to curse them, and bring destruction upon them; they must change, or else there is no

---

[9] Mosley, *Psychosophia*, 102-03.

Personal Applications and Pastoral Implications

repealing of the curse. The wicked hope he will change, the godly fear he will change.

Secondly, It comforts the godly, to whom he has made many promises, *Num.* 23:23. *Heb.* 13:5. He is constant and will perform them. He told *Adam, That the seed of the woman should break the Serpents head.* He was long, but sure, for it was fulfilled at last. *His Covenant is everlasting*, Isa. 55:3. *I am God and change not, therefore you are not consumed*, Mal. 3:6. we should labor for God's love, it is a freehold, and like himself, Immutable; *Whom he loves once, he loves forever.* God's people shall never fall from Grace, never be wholly overcome of Temptations.[10]

Conclusion

In conclusion, if you are outside of Christ, I declare to you that without doubt or deviation unless *you* are changed, unless you come to God in the righteousness of Christ Jesus, you will be judged, found guilty, condemned, and sent to everlasting punishment. But the good news of the gospel is that all those who trust in Christ Jesus, resting in and receiving his finished work, are most assuredly saved without any doubt or deviation. Trust in Jesus!

And, dear reader, if you are in Christ, take these truths with you and meditate upon them daily. Without any doubt or deviation, you will be vindicated on that final day of judgment, vindicated by perfect justice approving perfect righteousness, the righteousness of Christ. Therefore, "Let us hold fast the confession of our hope without wavering, *for he who promised is faithful*" (Heb 10:23). Remember that your foundation is the foundation of all things, God. Trust in

---

[10] Leigh, *A Systeme or Body of Divinity*, 181. Italics original.

God, trust in his promises, trust in his providence, and persevere. He will not change, and therefore you will not be consumed. Praise God in his immutable and impassible perfections.

Paul's words in Romans 8:38-39 are a fitting end to our study.

> For I am sure that neither death nor life, nor angels nor rulers, nor things present nor things to come, nor powers, [39] nor height nor depth, nor anything else in all creation, will be able to separate us from the love of God in Christ Jesus our Lord.

Amen!

Study Questions

1. How does the doctrine of divine impassibility affect your perseverance as a child of God?

2. If you are a child of God, and if you are going through trials and afflictions, does God love you?

3. How does the doctrine of divine impassibility affect the way that we preach the gospel?

4. Are you trusting in Jesus Christ for your salvation? If not, how does the doctrine of divine impassibility confront you in your sin?

5. If you are a believer in Jesus Christ, how does the doctrine of divine impassibility assure you of your salvation?

Personal Applications and Pastoral Implications

46813286R00064

Made in the USA
Lexington, KY
16 November 2015